DOWN BY THE LEMONADE SPRINGS

WESTERN LITERATURE SERIES

BOOKS BY JACKSON J. BENSON

....

Hemingway: The Writer's Art of Self-Defense (1969)

The True Adventures of John Steinbeck, Writer: A Biography (1984)

Looking for Steinbeck's Ghost (1989)

Wallace Stegner: His Life and Work (1996)

Wallace Stegner: A Study of the Short Fiction (1998)

Down by the Lemonade Springs: Essays on Wallace Stegner (2001)

DOWN BY THE
LEMONADE SPRINGS

··

ESSAYS ON WALLACE STEGNER

··

Jackson J. Benson ▲▲ *University of Nevada Press : Reno & Las Vegas*

WESTERN LITERATURE SERIES

University of Nevada Press, Reno, Nevada 89557 USA

Copyright © 1995, 1996, 1997, 1998, 2000, 2001 by

Jackson J. Benson

Manufactured in the United States of America

Design by Carrie House

Library of Congress Cataloging-in-Publication Data

Benson, Jackson J.

 Down by the lemonade springs : essays on Wallace

Stegner / Jackson J. Benson.

 p. cm. — (Western literature series)

Includes bibliographical references and index.

ISBN 0-87417-446-5 (alk. paper)

1. Stegner, Wallace Earle, 1909—Criticism and interpreta-

tion. 2. Western stories—History and criticism. 3. West

(U.S.)—In literature. I. Title. II. Series.

PS3537.T316 Z58 2001

813'.52—dc21   2001001408

The paper used in this book meets the requirements of

American National Standard for Information Sciences —

Permanence of Paper for Printed Materials, ANSI Z39.48-

1984. Binding materials were selected for strength and

durability.

Frontispiece: Wallace Stegner. Courtesy of Mary Stegner.

FIRST PRINTING

10 09 08 07 06 05 04 03 02 01

5 4 3 2 1

For Sydney Lynn Michaels

CONTENTS

Wallace Stegner died the evening of April 12, 1993, in Santa Fe, New Mexico, from injuries suffered in an auto accident two weeks earlier. During a long and distinguished career he received just about every award an American writer might receive, including a Pulitzer Prize for the 1971 novel *Angle of Repose* and a National Book Award in 1977 for *The Spectator Bird*. Among the many other tributes to him was a PEN Center West Freedom to Write Award given to him in the fall of 1992 to mark his refusal of the National Endowment for the Arts (NEA) medal, to have been presented by President George Bush, in order to protest the politicization of the NEA. In accepting the PEN Center award, Stegner wrote,

> I believe that government should support the arts. I also believe that its function stops with support—it has no business trying to direct or censor them. Art must be left to the artists. If they sometimes make mistakes, or press too hard, or test too strenuously the boundaries of the accepted, that is part of the commitment and the excitement: creation by definition deals with what has not yet been made. The creation of any art is three quarters error. As Lewis Thomas said, it was only by making mistakes that mankind blundered toward brains.

Born in Iowa, Wallace Stegner spent his childhood on the last homestead frontier in Saskatchewan and then the latter part of his life in the foothills of California—a remarkable span of time that ran from the horse-drawn plow to the information age. During Stegner's growing up, his father, a "boomer" looking to strike it rich, dragged the family from one place to another, finally—after an interim year in Great Falls, Montana—settling down for a few years as a bootlegger in Salt Lake City. A big, strong, violent man who tried to pursue frontier values in a postpioneer society, George Stegner became the basis for Bo Mason in *The Big Rock Candy Mountain* (1943), a novel that embodies the rootlessness, mobility, and rugged individualism that typified so much of western experience.

Wallace, physically weak as a child and scorned by his father, found acceptance in school and ended up working his way through the University of Utah and graduate school at the University of Iowa. He earned a Ph.D. in American literature, by contrast to his parents, who had not gone beyond the eighth grade, and went on to teach at Utah, Wisconsin, Harvard, and Stanford. He was a staff member for many years also at the granddaddy of all the summer writers' workshops, the Bread Loaf Writers' Conference in Vermont. It was there he met Robert Frost and Bernard DeVoto, both of whom would strongly influence his thought and writing (as I will describe in more detail in later essays).

During the late 1930s, the 1940s, and the early 1950s, he became known as an outstanding short-story writer. One of his stories appeared in the annual *The Best American Short Stories* in each of the successive years 1941–1943, and "Two Rivers" won second prize in the 1942 O. Henry competition. Over the next three decades one of his stories was included in the *Best* series on six more occasions, and he made four more appearances in the *O. Henry Memorial Award Prize Stories*, including another second prize, for "Beyond the Glass Mountain" (1947), and a first prize for "The Blue-Winged Teal" (1950).

He was a man, to paraphrase what Robert Stone has said about one of his characters in a recent novel, who practiced the virtues that most of us used to believe in—kindness, courtesy, responsibility, and hard work. He had many roles—novelist, essayist, historian, lecturer, editor, and environmentalist—but perhaps all of them go back to one central role, as I will point out in my introduction, that of teacher. As teacher in the formal sense, he is known for founding Stanford University's creative writing program, which he directed for twenty-five years, producing several dozen of our most accomplished writers. As teacher in a less formal sense, he was all his life a truth seeker who tried to see himself, his history, his land, and his people as clearly as possible and to pass on those discoveries to others.

As a Westerner who frequently wrote about western subjects, he worked to increase our understanding of the West—its history, its geography, and its social dynamics—and to expose the myths that all too often had contributed to its exploitation. He was a writer shaped in large part by his sense of the importance of history. Most of what he wrote, beyond the histories themselves, whether fiction, biography, or essay, employed history as part of his perspective.

This attachment to history and his drive to learn about it in various contexts seem to have come out of his own experience. He felt in growing up that he had been cut away from his roots, that he had no history as a basis for understanding his own life. Like Bruce Mason, his semi-autobiographical persona in *The Big Rock Candy Mountain,* Stegner came to think of his family as an outlaw family, always secretive, always on the run, and never in tune with neighbors or community, except for a time during the winters in Saskatchewan. This isolation gave Stegner a need to belong, to find a place that he could relate to and a tradition to be a part of. It also planted in him a life-long admiration for the community-building that he witnessed as a teenager among the Mormons in Salt Lake City.

In his Mormon histories, *Mormon Country* (1942) and *The Gathering of Zion* (1964; winner of the 1965 Award of Merit of the American Association for State and Local History), Stegner displayed the fallacy of a West created by the lone horseman, and demonstrated how important cooperation was to its actual development. His biography of John Wesley Powell, *Beyond the Hundredth Meridian* (1954), performed the invaluable service of reminding us that the West was not a New Eden, a paradise, but for the most part an arid, near desert. His biography of Bernard DeVoto, *The Uneasy Chair* (1974), did much to spread the DeVoto gospel concerning the need to preserve public lands and the need for constant public vigilance in their protection. With these latter two works alone he made a substantial contribution to the emergence, development, and agenda of the environmental movement.

In *Wolf Willow* (1962), he recreated the environment of his own roots in Saskatchewan on the last of the homestead frontiers through the combination of a history, a memoir, and a fictional account of the cattle-ranching disaster of the winter of 1906–7. These two stories, "Genesis" and "Carrion Spring," were the only "cowboy" stories he ever wrote. Growing up, he frequently came into contact with the real thing, and in his introduction to the two stories he wrote about their influence, for better and worse, on him:

> Many things those cowboys represented I would have done well to get over quickly, or never catch: the prejudice, the callousness, the destructive practical joking, the tendency to judge everyone by the same raw standard. Nevertheless, what they themselves most respected, and what as a boy I most yearned to grow up to, was as noble as it was limited. They honored courage, competence, self-reliance, and they honored them tacitly. They took them for granted. It was their absence, not their presence, that was cause for remark. Practicing comradeship in a rough and dangerous job, they lived a life calculated to make a man careless of everything except the few things he really valued. (*Wolf Willow* 136)

As an environmentalist, Wallace Stegner was well known for his activities on behalf of the Sierra Club and the Wilderness Society, as well as for his many publications on the subject. Among these was "Wilderness Letter" (1961), which defined wilderness as "the geography of hope":

> Something will have gone out of us as a people if we ever let the remaining wilderness be destroyed; if we permit the last virgin forests to be turned into comic books and plastic cigarette cases; if we drive the few remaining members of the wild species into zoos or to extinction. . . . Never again will Americans be free in their own country from the noise, the exhausts, the stinks of human and automotive waste. . . . And . . . never again can we have the chance to see ourselves single, separate, vertical and individual in the world, part of the environment of trees and rocks and soil, brother to the other animals, part of the natural world and competent to belong in it. (*The Sound* 146–47)

In 1969 he published his first collection of essays, *The Sound of Mountain Water,* which included "Wilderness Letter" and which certified him as a leading commentator, both lovingly and skeptically, on the West and western experience. In his introduction to the collection, he is already striking a note of caution and concern:

> If these essays begin in innocence, with a simple-minded love of western
> landscapes and western experience, they move toward the attempt, more
> systematically made in other books of mine, to understand what it is
> one loves, what is special or fragile about it, and how far love will take
> us. It is possible to love a country to death. (10–11)

In that same introduction he notes that "*limitation, deprivation,* are words
we must keep in mind when speaking of the reputedly limitless West" (10).

In more recent years, he joined with his son, Page, to write *American Places*
(1981), using his extensive knowledge of the exploration, exploitation, and
topography of our land to put forth one of the finest books on our complex
and generally destructive relationship to our continent. In 1982 he published
his third collection of essays, *One Way to Spell Man,* and in 1986, 1987, and
1988 he published three series of lectures, *The Sense of Place, The American
West as Living Space,* and *On the Teaching of Creative Writing,* respectively. His
last novel, *Crossing to Safety,* came out in 1987, and his *Collected Stories* in
1990. His last publication before his death was a fourth collection of essays,
*Where the Bluebird Sings to the Lemonade Springs: Living and Writing in the
West* (1992). A final collection, edited by his son, Page, was published posthu-
mously in 1998: *Marking the Sparrow's Fall: Wallace Stegner's American West.*

For those who knew Wallace Stegner personally, his loss is particularly
difficult to bear. Everyone I knew who knew him expected him to always be
there, like a national monument, weathered, craggy, and inspirational—an
image carved in stone on a mountain. In a way, his finest work of art was
himself. He often declared that his motive for writing was to examine himself, his roots, his motives and goals. Out of that self-examination, and a
constant determination to grow, came one of the most remarkable persons
of this or any other time. No man ever had more integrity. We in the West
can take him, in death, to our hearts to cherish as one of ours, the best of
what we can be. But we can also with some pride present him to the world, a
great man and a great American writer.

In the essays that follow, I examine the man and his work and the connections between the two. In the case of Wallace Stegner, whose fiction was
usually autobiographical, the connections were close and frequent. I look at
the evolution of his fiction, how at the middle of his career he found his
"voice," and I look at the circumstances that led him to become a spokesman

for the environmental movement. I evaluate his environmentalism and discuss his philosophy and values, as well as the sources of those values in his experiences and friendships. I take a look at his work for racial equality and for understanding between races. In all of these discussions I approach the subjects from the point of view of a biographer. The essays were written over a period of ten years, most published in various journals as noted in the acknowledgments, and written to explore various aspects of the writer in more detail than space would allow in my Stegner biography.

ACKNOWLEDGMENTS

"Where the Old West Met the New—Wallace Stegner: 1909–1993" was originally published in *Montana: The Magazine of Western History.* Several of the anecdotes in "A Teacher for All Seasons" appeared previously in the introduction to my biography, *Wallace Stegner: His Life and Work.* "Writing as the Expression of Belief" was originally published in *Wallace Stegner and the Continental Vision,* edited by Curt Meine. "The Battle against Rugged Individualism" first appeared in the *North Dakota Quarterly;* "Artist as Environmentalist" in *Value and Vision in American Literature,* edited by Joseph Candido; "Finding a Voice of His Own: The Story of Wallace Stegner's Fiction" in *Western American Literature;* "A Friendship with Consequences: Robert Frost and Wallace Stegner" in the *South Dakota Review;* and "'Eastering': Wallace Stegner's Love Affair with Vermont" in *Western American Literature.* "The Short Stories: The College Years" is taken from "Stories Related to the College Years" in my *Wallace Stegner: A Study of the Short Fiction.* "An Introduction to Wallace Stegner's *Angle of Repose*" is from the Penguin Classics edition of the novel.

Quotations from the published and unpublished works of Wallace Stegner are used with the permission of Mary Stegner.

A Teacher for All Seasons

I first met Wallace Stegner in 1986. I had called him to ask if I could discuss doing a book about him. He had written a generous review of my Steinbeck biography for the *Los Angeles Times*, and I was looking for a new project. The idea was appealing, for although I had read only a few of Stegner's novels and his nonfiction *Beyond the Hundredth Meridian*, I had admired and enjoyed his work. More importantly perhaps, I felt I shared many of his values, and although I had only sketchy information about his life, I admired him for what he had been able to accomplish coming out of an impoverished background.

His seemed to be a real-life Horatio Alger story, except that rather than having achieved riches, he had spent his life creating art and serving others, writing and teaching. Also, by choosing to write about him, I felt I was continuing in a direction I had already been taking, for he had several things in common with Steinbeck. They were both Westerners, they were known for their integrity, they had a strong sense of place and a concern for the environment, and they had both either been looked down upon or ignored by the eastern intellectual press.

Many years ago, when I was in undergraduate classes in creative writing at Stanford, I saw him from a distance and heard him speak on several occasions. In those days, whenever he brought a distinguished writer to campus to speak to his seminar, he would gather together all the creative writing classes, graduate and undergraduate, in a lecture hall to hear the writer speak. He would introduce the speaker on each occasion—certainly helpful in my case, since in those days of innocence and ignorance I had no idea who any of them were. I do not remember anything that Wallace Stegner said, but I do remember vividly a man of striking appearance—tall, broad-shouldered, with penetrating blue eyes and metal-rimmed glasses, and most memorable of all, that shock of nearly white hair. Now, as I met him for the first time, some thirty-five years later, I was taken aback to see that he had changed hardly at all.

When he met me at the door, I noticed that he was still tall and robust-looking, with erect posture. He was seventy-seven but looked to be in his early sixties. He was wearing khakis and a freshly ironed, short-sleeved shirt. He looked crisp and relaxed—I was perspiring. We sat out in the sun on the brick patio in front of his house in Los Altos Hills surrounded by a profusion of oak trees and shrubs and the flowering vines that blocked off the view of the house from the driveway. He must have noticed that I was suffering from the heat and from nervousness, for he went over and turned on the fountain and offered me some fruit juice.

I knew enough of his fame and reputation to be intimidated by him, but Wally (it was not long after our first meeting that he insisted that I call him Wally) put me at ease almost at once. He seemed genuinely pleased that I should want to write about him and told me that he had been impressed by my work. There was nothing arrogant in his manner—he treated me with the casual courtesy and plain speech he would have used with an equal, and I found myself liking him almost immediately. I told him that I wanted to write a biography, but that I would not go ahead without his permission and cooperation.

He responded by making it clear that although he was happy to have books written about him, he was not comfortable at all with the idea of biography as it was usually written nowadays. He referred to the biographies that he had written, about John Wesley Powell and Bernard DeVoto, and stated that he had avoided personal details and had concentrated only on these men's careers and hoped I would do the same. I told him I would do my best but could not promise that the book would not include something he might object to. He smiled and said that the book might well come out after his death (he was aware that my Steinbeck biography had taken thir-teen years of research and writing, so that my track record for speed was not impressive) and that he would trust my judgment about what to say and what to leave out.

This was not the only occasion when I observed his prickly sense of privacy, overly developed, I thought, considering his life of almost unblemished probity. I once complained to Tom Watkins of the Wilderness Society, telling him that considering the virtuous life that Stegner had led, I could not understand why he should be so concerned about my somehow violating his privacy. Watkins reminded me, "Don't forget—he's Norwegian."

Although I eventually discovered that he had had an eventful and, to a large extent, unusual life, I worried at the beginning that there might not be much high drama. After all, he had been married to the same woman for more than fifty years, was not a boozer or womanizer, had no bizarre habits, and had not shot or stabbed anyone. During the course of interviewing his friends, I expressed this same concern to Wally's longtime friend Joe Houghteling, and he gave me the line that became a joke between Wally and me. If I got stumped for something to spice up the book, I could, Wally would tell me with a twinkle in his eye, always tell about the night in Paris when he knocked down Ernest Hemingway.

Wally was so straight that despite a story filled with achievement and adventure, his life might seem comparatively dull to some—particularly those conditioned by a *National Inquirer* public mentality—except for his sense of humor. Many of his letters are sprinkled with it, as was his conversation. He was a man who took himself seriously and yet could poke fun at himself for taking himself so seriously. He saw clearly the absurdities of life around him, and no one was more aware of the follies of the local and national political scenes. He loved to play with words—puns, rhymes, and verses flowed effortlessly from his mouth when a playful mood struck him. His sense of humor was wry (I am forced to employ that overused term), playful, puckish, and sometimes sly. He knew hundreds of songs and poems by heart (ranging from Chaucer and Milton to Dickinson and Frost) and would recite Robert Service and reams of Don Marquis when he knew you well enough and the subject at hand triggered a recitation. He had worked so hard, accomplished so much, and held himself to such a strict standard of conduct throughout his life that it might appear to the casual observer that he was rather stern and unbending—old sober sides.

But for decades he could be the life of any party, and his wife, Mary, remembers many an evening that ended with Wally standing at the piano, in his shirtsleeves and with glass in hand, singing in his fine, strong voice any old favorite that might have been requested. His good friend Claude Simpson, who had been at Wisconsin and Harvard and was now at Stanford with him, would be at the keyboard, an English professor but also a musical genius who could play anything, his sleeves rolled up, his collar open, and the butt of a cigar clenched between his teeth.

No one who had so much energy right up until his mid-eighties could ever be dull—his level of activity throughout his life was amazing. When I was with him, he was nearly always working on several things at the same time, planning trips, and arranging a complicated speaking schedule. Unlike most of us reacting to such a load, he never seemed rushed, panicky, or nervous. He seemed so . . . so reliable, so much like the Rock of Gibraltar, that when he left us, it was difficult for those of us who knew him to believe that he was gone.

He was a man who never had a clean plate, and it did not seem to bother him at all. With all his activity, he never seemed to resent the time it took to sit down with me and be interviewed, sometimes hours a day for more than a week at a time. I never heard him complain, even though he was stricken in his later years by a variety of illnesses. The closest he ever came to that was when I wrote to him about my mother breaking her hip, and he wrote back, "I am sorry about your mother. The joys of getting old are perennial and as numerous as the sands of the sea." Having lived until his mid-eighties and having earlier in life tended for months his mother, who was dying a painful death from cancer, and suffered the death of three close women friends from cancer, he knew about aging, illness, and death and was one of the few major writers of our time to write candidly and frequently about these things.

Like the work of one of his mentors, Robert Frost, his writing had both a sunny and a dark side, and he was never sentimental. What he said about Frost was just as true for him: "The real jolt and force of Frost's love of life comes from the fact that it is cold at the root." He tried mightily to face life directly, unflinchingly, and to be completely honest both in his living and his writing. As his colleague Nancy Packer said once about him, he felt strongly that creating a work of fiction was the expression of belief. He also felt strongly that the good man living the good life was a product of right conduct—he held no truck with those who spoke always of "behavior," that is, action without thought or a sense of responsibility.

I spent several weeks a year, off and on, with him for nearly seven years, first interviewing him and then going over his papers in his home office, and I found myself impressed not only with his energy but with his sense of purpose. I could be sitting at a table in his office early in the morning reading through some letters, and after asking if I were comfortable, he would turn to his old upright typewriter and stay with it for hours. While I would take numerous breaks to walk in the yard or go to the bathroom, he would be still banging away. He had incredible powers of concentration. Unlike every other famous person I had run into over the years, Wally always had his phone number listed in the directory, and the phone would ring now and again all morning. Usually Mary answered it, if she was home, and fended off requests, but on several occasions I witnessed him stop what he was doing and answer the phone himself. He was always polite, never irritated or dismissive, but usually declined the offer to speak or to write something—often an introduction to someone else's book (in a moment of uncharacteristic exasperation, he turned to me on one occasion and claimed to be the champion introduction writer of all time). Then he would swing back to the typewriter as if he had not missed a beat.

He was simply the brightest man I had ever known. He was always two steps ahead of me, and I sometimes did not understand the implications of what he had said until I had gotten home, sat down, and had a chance to think it over. But what made his intelligence even more impressive was an incredible memory, a vast amount of general knowledge (especially knowledge of the background and geology of places, but he had also taught English and American literature from *Beowulf* to the present day, was an expert on western literature and history, and had gained, largely from his wife, a good deal of knowledge about art and music). If ever there was a Renaissance man, it was he. And it might surprise some to know that although he was an intellectual, he had been an athlete in college and loved to watch sports on TV. He was until the end a reader and a learner and always behind, as he admitted to me, not knowing as much as he should know. No doubt his superb intellectual equipment was in large part responsible for the almost unbelievable depth and range of his accomplishments. It also made his lack of arrogance and his patience and invariable kindness to others that much more remarkable.

The downside was that he was not only prickly about matters he considered too private or in some way a negative reflection on his integrity (usually things that I did not consider negative at all) but also sensitive about anything that might reflect badly on his performance of his responsibilities. He was a man of duty, even in the smallest of things. No one could be more conscientious in his practice of courtesy, and after he agreed to cooperate with me, he considered one of his duties was to arrange for my comfort. When I came to work, he would have a table, its top cleared of papers and books, and a chair with a cushion all set up for me—through all our years together he never forgot to do this. If I worked through lunchtime, he would arrange to feed me if he was home and did not have guests.

It was a joy to be in his company even if a lot of the time, during the last years when I was reading his papers, we sat ten feet apart and ignored each other. Sometimes, however, especially in the early mornings while warming our hands at the little Danish fireplace in his office, we talked. Current events during the late 1980s and Ronald Reagan's active hostility to the environment were particularly depressing for him. There were things that really bothered him, such as the Sagebrush Rebellion ("The Western states never did own that land") and our inability in the West to understand our region's aridity; and he would come back again and again to these topics.

His conversation was peppered with references to the two men who had had such an influence on him early in his career, Robert Frost and Bernard DeVoto, and he referred on a number of occasions to the two fiction writers he seemed to admire most, Anton Chekhov and Joseph Conrad. He once told Nancy Packer that writers could be divided into two camps, those who admired Chekhov and those who admired Tolstoy, and that he was a Chekhov man himself.

As time came to start writing the biography, I searched for some central theme. Wallace Stegner had excelled in so many activities, had given so much of himself to so many in so many various ways, and had written so many different kinds of things, it was hard for me to think of what might tie these things all together. What was the common denominator?

One answer came to me on an afternoon in Arizona while interviewing Stewart Udall. I had made it a practice as I traveled around the country interviewing Wally's friends, colleagues, and former students to ask each of them, "If you were writing this book, what would be your theme—what would be your central point about this man?" Some, like Wendell Berry, said that they thought it was his growing up on the frontier and the resulting intimate connection with the land that was at the heart of what he was and what he wrote. Others, like James Houston, pointed to his integrity, which they felt gave his life and his work a special quality;[1] unlike so many other writers Stegner never resorted to sensational material to sell books or cheap tricks to gain publicity. Stewart Udall surprised me. He said he thought that Wally at heart was a very special kind of teacher. Determined to declare the truth as he saw it and serve others, Wally was a teacher in everything he did, whether actually teaching writing, writing fiction or nonfiction, or working to save the environment. That was what in Udall's mind tied it together. All the answers to my question were good ones, but his may have been the best.

CHAPTER ONE

Writing as the Expression of Belief

On a number of occasions, Wallace Stegner said that for him fiction was "dramatized belief." His former student and friend, Nancy Packer, has observed that "some writers are interested only in the aesthetics of writing, but for Wally, writing is a moral act. He deeply cared about what it means to live in a complex world" (Packer 1). He was a man of integrity, and what he wrote, both fiction and nonfiction, reflected that integrity. What made him stand out from other writers of his time was that his life and his work were so much of one piece. In life he was unpretentious, observant, and always, even in old age, learning. In connection with these qualities, he devoted much of his writing to the job of getting behind the myth, behind pretentiousness and deception, to find the truth. He was the ultimate realist. "In fiction," he wrote, "we should have no agenda except to try to be truthful" ("Law" 222). His search was uncompromising.

He believed in those things we used to believe in—enduring love, friendship, generosity, kindness, fairness, duty, and sacrifice. These were the things he wrote about in an age when they have been so often debased, discounted, or ignored—or even mocked as old-fashioned or irrelevant. He was really one of a kind, a voice in the wilderness, a writer who we can treasure if we value the things he valued. He had no truck with talk about behavior, but would talk only about conduct. He insisted that there *was* a difference.

While he was a man of compassion, a liberal in the best sense of the word, he could not abide self-pity or a preoccupation with blame, for he had been there himself. He had been the victim, he had been abused, and he had felt put-upon, but he came to reject that mode of thinking in his own life and to despise it in others. "Only by repudiating the buck-passing irresponsibility of our period," he wrote, "can a man assert anything like his full dignity as an individual" ("Variations on a Theme by Conrad" 521). No contemporary writer was ever less sentimental while at the same time frequently writing about those things we are inclined to be sentimental about—love, kindness, charity, and forgiveness.

His realism is sometimes so bitter-tasting that it is difficult for the reader to swallow. Just as he was hard on himself, he was hard on his fictional creations. For him life was a test of character. When one reads *The Big Rock Candy Mountain* or *Angle of Repose*, one has the definite feeling over and over again that something bad is going to happen and, sure enough, over and over again it does. That feeling makes it hard to pursue a long novel with enthusiasm. Stegner recognized this quality in his work: "I don't think I'm a particularly jovial or genial writer. I think a lot of my books are glum, bleak even" (Dillon 57). He attributed this bleakness to his own habit of mind, which tended to be skeptical and pessimistic. Like Mark Twain he was a disillusioned romantic who found some merriment in human foibles but in his heart was constantly disappointed by human behavior—its intolerance, its self-centeredness, its self-deceptions, its rapacious misuse of the land. As he grew older, like Twain he became more and more pessimistic about mankind and its future, or as he put it, "I walk behind the times muttering about the way things are going" (Hanscom 18). He once admitted that as a realist he probably would have been better suited to have lived and written in the nineteenth century along with Twain and Henry James.

He also freely admitted distaste for much, but not all, contemporary writing: "I think now books are unfortunately pretty well riddled with what used to have a shock value, which means it has to have a higher voltage to shock now. . . . It's kind of a disease: attempting to be clever, sexy or violent. It's a way of showing off" (Mills n. pag.). When asked once by writer Sean O'Faolain how he managed to avoid being trendy, Stegner replied, "I write the kind of novel I can write. I don't know how to write out of the headlines" (Hanscom 18). When an interviewer in effect accused him of lacking originality and innovation and cited *Angle of Repose* as an "extremely traditional novel," he replied that that label did not bother him one bit:

I don't really aspire to write a novel which can be read backwards as well as forward, which turns chronology on its head and has no continuity and no narrative, which, in effect, tries to create a novel by throwing all the pieces in the bag and shaking the bag. . . . If you have to do *that* to be original, then I don't care about being original. (Hepworth 9)

Not only did he have similarities of temperament with Mark Twain, but also his career and his writing had a number of things in common with those of the master, Henry James. Like James, he had a major success in mid-career. For James it was *Portrait of a Lady*; for Stegner, *The Big Rock Candy Mountain*, which has taken its place among the classic novels of western experience. Both writers got better as they got older; James reaching the pinnacle of his powers with his late novels, Stegner reaching toward greatness with his last four: *All the Little Live Things, Angle of Repose, The Spectator Bird*, and *Crossing to Safety*. Both writers wrote novels with very little plot; they tended to build dramatic situations that are realized internally rather than depending on dramatic actions. Their fictions were less, in Stegner's words, "a complication resolved than what Henry James was to call a 'situation revealed'" (W. Stegner and M. Stegner 15). The two writers emphasized nuance of thought and emotion and were masters of the indeterminate, ironic ending—the kind of ending that stays with you and makes you think back on everything that led up to it.

Who could ever forget the conclusion of James's *The Wings of the Dove*? Densher and Kate develop a cynical plan to get the dying Milly Theale's money by having her fall in love with Densher. But when Densher, against his own will, becomes very fond of her, the game changes. After Milly dies and Densher receives a legacy from her, which he declines, he turns to Kate and assures her that they will be as they were. "As we were?" she asks. "As we were," he replies (512). But the reader shares their bitter knowledge that fortune has turned the tables on them and that their relationship can never be the same. As we were? What would make anyone believe that Kate would want to go back or that Densher's lack of fortune no longer mattered to her?

Or can we forget the ending of *Angle of Repose*, where Lyman Ward lies in bed thinking, listening to the trucks laboring up the long grade on the highway near his Grass Valley home and wondering if he could possibly send for and thus forgive his unfaithful wife? "Wisdom, I said oh so glibly the other day . . . is knowing what you have to accept. In this not-quite-quiet darkness, while the diesel breaks its heart more and more faintly on the mountain grade, I lie wondering if I am man enough to be a bigger man than my grandfather" (569). Can the human heart ever be restored? Can things ever be as they were?

Both writers were concerned with the function of point of view in their fiction. It became a priority for Stegner only slowly, after considerable thought and some trial and error. In one of his interviews with Richard Etulain he said, "Over a period of many years I have come to think point of view the most important basic problem in the writing of fiction" (Stegner and Etulain 64). In class he used the image of a garden hose running with a nozzle and without a nozzle: "You get," he would tell his students, "more force with a nozzle." That nozzle changed for him over time. He began using almost exclusively a strictly limited, Jamesian point of view, that variation of the third person we call "center of consciousness." He admired the way that James, over the course of his career, limited his point of view more and more, so that as "he forced his story through smaller and smaller outlets, . . . it acquired a special concentration and force" (W. Stegner and M. Stegner 16). But Stegner discovered that there were subtleties in point of view "that Henry himself didn't know about. You don't have to be as rigid as he, and yet point of view is just as important, maybe even more important then he thought it was" (Stegner and Etulain 64). The irony is that he achieved his own greatness by turning away from that James model to the use of the first-person narrative, something that James had never used. It gave him many advantages he did not have before, but it also held some dangers.

With Joe Allston, in "A Field Guide to the Western Birds" to begin with and then *All the Little Live Things*, followed in the last novels by his first-person counterparts, Lyman Ward and Larry Morgan, Stegner invented the grumpy old man, with his humor and pathos, long before he was discovered by Jack Lemmon and Walter Matthau. When asked by an interviewer why he used Joe Allston, Stegner replied half jokingly, "I liked the chance to be crabby if I felt like being crabby and put it inside somebody else's mouth" (Bonnetti). But the first person also had many technical advantages. Stegner found he could do some things he could hardly do by other means: it "encourages you to syncopate time . . . [and] allows you to drop back and forth, almost at will, freely" (Stegner and Etulain 78). Interpenetrating the past and the present, which he does frequently in these final novels, was important to him as a writer who was also a historian, someone who became a historian because he felt keenly the lack of knowledge about his own past. He admired Faulkner for the richness of his associations from the past and mourned the poverty of these associations in most western novels.

Stegner found that the first person brought him closer to his work than ever before and gave him freedom, allowing him to be pretty much himself or to do or say pretty much what he might imagine himself doing or saying, while speaking through a mask the way Conrad speaks through Marlowe. That is to say it allowed him to dramatize more directly and effectively his beliefs. Yet Stegner had avoided that technique for years because he was afraid it might lead him to be windy, and he was afraid—as a very private man—of revealing too much of himself inadvertently. His fear of revealing himself, or seeming to reveal himself, was justified, and he tried mightily to persuade his audience that although he contributed much to them, he was not identical to his first-person narrators. Nevertheless, the reader's identification of author with speaker was almost inevitable.

Stegner treated this confusion of writer and character with humor at times and at other times with irritation. On the one hand, he thought it amusing when was doing the book tour for *Crossing to Safety* that so many in his audiences were surprised to see that his wife, Mary, was not wearing braces. On the other hand, he would become irritated with me as his biographer when I asked questions about models for his characters or about the factual background for any of his works. He was as cognizant as I was that these questions were the things that readers of biography are most interested in, and I thought that his irritation was somewhat disingenuous, especially since sometimes in public he would talk freely (as he had on occasion written freely) about sources of material in his own life and about opinions that he and his narrators shared.

Regardless of his occasional protests, it is clear that the man and his work were joined together closely in any number of ways. The fact is, of course, that most of his work is autobiographical, and at times he would admit this but state that his life was the only material available for him to draw on as a writer. The point for him was that although it may have been his life, the material of that life was changed, given form and direction. It did not matter how autobiographical his work was, he protested: "Both fiction and autobiography attempt to impose order on the only life the writer really knows, his own" ("The Law" 219). The point for us is the recognition of how closely his life and work were joined: it is a matter not of the narrator's identity but of his values and beliefs.

The metaphor that he used for this artistic process was the lens. In an essay on his philosophy of writing, he wrote:

> One page or six hundred, a fiction is more than a well-carpentered entertainment. It is also more than the mirror in the roadway that Stendhal said it was. Because a good writer is not really a mirror; he is a lens. One mirror is like another, a mechanical reflector, but a lens may be anything from what is in your Instamatic to what makes you handle your Hasselblad with reverence. Ultimately there is no escaping the fact that fiction is only as good as its maker. It sees only with the clarity that he is capable of, and it perpetuates his astigmatisms. ("The Law" 217)

What, then, were the properties given to this lens, and what were the characteristics of its images? What were the aspects of Wallace Stegner that produced the fiction that dramatized his beliefs and whose qualities we admire? First, certain unique experiences while growing up; second, an enormous talent; third, an incredible self-discipline; and fourth, a lifelong thirst for learning, which resulted in an unusual breadth of knowledge. Alone among the major writers of his time, Stegner lived a life that almost spanned the century, which gave him an unusually long perspective. Growing up on a farm on the last homestead frontier immersed him early in nature and gave him an intuitive appreciation of the importance of human-kind's relationship to the earth and planted the seed for his appreciation of a sense of place as a basis for his fiction. He repeatedly confirmed the impor-tance of that appreciation, as when he said, "I don't think you can be a decent novelist without having a sense of place. I know some novelists who don't have it, and it seems to me that without knowing it, it's like a vitamin deficiency" (Rideout 13).

Mocked for his smallness and sickliness as a child and abused by a brutish father, Stegner learned to stick things out and not complain. He grew up to be a gentle man but also a tough man, without any self-pity and without a sentimental bone in his body. Alone much of the time as a child on the farm and then isolated as a teenager because of his father's outlaw status, he found his comfort in books, his only approval coming from his mother and teachers for his school work. He became a voracious reader and was an outstanding student throughout his school and college years. He resented his father's rugged individualism and pursuit of the get-rich-quick western dream and in reaction supported and advocated throughout his writing career the importance of cooperation and spirit of community; family and friends were important to him, and these were among his primary subjects.

Stegner's writing talent was far greater than we have yet generally appreciated. Early on he learned to love literature and love the sound of words. He had a remarkable gift for remembering poetry and verse, and that in turn led to the development of a discriminating ear for the rhythms of prose. Those who knew him well have testified that metaphor was a habit of mind that came out even in ordinary conversation. He had what he, himself, in talking about others called "sensibility." In an essay he wrote for *Saturday Review* about judging student writers, he declared that sensibility was essential for a writer, and even "though [it] . . . can be trained and sharpened, it cannot be created or acquired." Rather than being one of those, as in Henry James's famous advice, on whom nothing is lost, Stegner declared that he "should like to be one who seizes from everything *some* vivid impression," for "there ought to be a poet submerged in every novelist" ("Sensibility" 24).

On sheer talent, without knowing much, if anything, about storytelling technique, he sat down and wrote his first long manuscript and won a major prize for it. Perhaps the best testimony to his talent would be the opening paragraph of one of his earliest short stories, "Bugle Song," which he wrote in 1937 during his first year teaching at the University of Wisconsin. I mention its earliness to emphasize the native talent of the writer who produced it—Stegner considered it his first professional story. This opening paragraph illustrates that no one has been better able than Stegner, even at the beginning of his career, to create an atmosphere, a mood, or to subtly suggest a condition of the soul or spirit by providing a suggestive landscape:

There had been a wind during the night, and all the loneliness of the world had swept up out of the southwest. The boy had heard it wailing through the screens of the sleeping porch where he lay, and he had heard the washtub bang loose from the outside wall and roll down toward the coulee, and the slam of the screen doors, and his mother's padding feet after she rose to fasten things down. Through one half-open eye he had peered up from his pillow to see the moon skimming windily in a luminous sky; in his mind he had seen the prairie outside with its woolly grass and cactus white under the moon, and the wind, whining across that endless oceanic land, sang in the screens, and sang him back to sleep. (13)

Indirectly, metaphorically, the paragraph introduces the thematic conflicts of the story: untamed nature and frontier values versus domesticity and the values of civilization. But beyond what the paragraph accomplishes in brief space thematically, what strikes us most immediately is its haunting beauty, which comes out of its imagery and its nearly perfect rhythmic patterning. What we have here is part and parcel of what the author was—his childhood experience and sense of place, his metaphorical imagination, and his sensitivity to language.

Talent is important, but just as important is the self-discipline with which that talent is developed and applied. While he was teaching first at Utah and then at Wisconsin, Stegner had a ten o'clock class every day, and since he had already decided he would be a writer as well as a teacher, he would write every morning starting at seven and then rush off up the hill to class a little before ten (both campuses were on hills, and the trip to class provided his exercise for the day). This began a routine, which he followed during the rest of his life, of sitting down to write early every morning; and when he was not teaching, he extended the session to the early afternoon. Whether the writing was going well or not going at all, he stuck with it, not letting himself get up from his chair until his session was over. That perseverance was for him the basis for being a professional—staying with it. By the time he went to Harvard, after Wisconsin had refused to promote him, his wife was worried much of the time about his health because he worked such long hours and spent so little time resting.

Amazingly, his strict work ethic never abated—even at retirement age he never slowed down. He simply left his post as head of Stanford's creative writing program in order to devote more time to his own writing. Several days after he died of injuries in a car accident at the age of eighty-four, his wife, Mary, went out to clean out his office and put things in order. Over his desk, pinned to the wall, she found a handwritten list of ten items that he had been planning to write in the weeks following his trip to Santa Fe—articles, speeches, and introductions.

Although my description has emphasized his strict moral standards and stern self-discipline, I should note once again that like most very bright people, he had a wonderfully witty and playful sense of humor. He was interested in many things, from geology to sports, from Native American history to classical music, from the cooperative movement to conservation. He was a reader, a learner all his life, and whether he was at graduate school at Iowa or teaching at Utah, Wisconsin, Harvard, or Stanford, he always thought he was behind, that his colleagues knew much more than he, and that he would have to work like hell to get caught up. And he did—worked like hell and got caught up.

His superb intellectual equipment undoubtedly was in large part responsible for the depth and range of his accomplishments. He had ground and polished a lens, applying the grit of experience and self-discipline to the raw materials of talent and intelligence to produce images, a body of work, that had a more consistent quality and a wider variety than that of any other writer of his time. In addition to awards for his novels, his histories, and his short stories, he was presented later in his career with a half dozen lifetime achievement awards. In his case, to a large extent, the man *was* his work— his was a lifetime spent in honesty, realism, and dedication to the truth. He was a good deal more like the stereotypical western hero than he would have ever admitted—he was one tough customer. And notice, I smile when I say that.

CHAPTER TWO

The Battle Against Rugged Individualism

There are several strands of realism in twentieth-century American fiction, and of these, probably the most persistent and enduring is that which seeks to refute the illusions we attempt to live by, both as individuals and as a society. In this mode, realism is essentially moralistic, for it suggests that the illusions that we hold so dear are the sources of many of our social ills, allowing us to avoid problems and to become self-righteously judgmental. We are great avoiders (revenue enhancement is permitted, but taxes are forbidden), and we are great pretenders: we have found it far more convenient and pleasant to live our lives according to a mythology and to follow maps that have little to do with the actual territory.

It is this fundamental characteristic of American culture that has prompted many of our writers to continue to follow the path of realism, even though the avant-garde several decades ago declared it passé in favor of other modes— metafiction, fabulation, and magic realism, the uses of fantasy made popular by Central and South American writers. Fantasy, however, is the problem in our culture, and as a culture, we probably need a stronger sense of reality for our writing to have the ironic impact it has in eastern Europe or South America, where reality, for most, is all too present and overwhelming. In short, as moralists, fiction writers often seem to use fantasy to criticize reality, and strong doses of reality to criticize an addiction to fantasy.

One writer who bucked the trends and ignored the fads to remain a realist and has been criticized for it as being "out-of-date" is Wallace Stegner. The one myth above all that Stegner, as a realist, sought throughout his career to expose as false and dangerous is our cultural doctrine of "rugged individualism." That refutation can be seen at the center of nearly all of his work, as novelist, historian, and environmentalist. And since rugged individualism has found many of its signatures in western lore—the Marlboro man—it is fitting that it has been largely western writers—Stegner, along with A. B. Guthrie, Walter Clark, and John Steinbeck—who have refuted the western romances of Luke Short, Louis L'Amour, and Hollywood with such vigor. Stegner, as I pointed out earlier, is a western writer who wrote only two cowboy stories in his long and prolific career.[1]

The implications of the myth of rugged individualism run deep into our culture.[2] It is this doctrine that has provided our archetype for manhood, the cowboy with his six-shooter (or one of his descendents, Rambo with his AK-47) that most young boys are led to emulate starting at three or four years old. They learn to exclude girls from their play as incompetent, and they are taught by their culture—usually regardless of what their parents may advocate—that violence is an essential part of the masculine role. Our love of guns runs deep, since it defines who we, as males, are. It is the myth of rugged, self-sufficient individualism that has led us to be so intolerant of those who are weak and dependent and as a nation to have such an abiding hatred of welfare. Any individual, if he or she just has enough faith and works hard enough, can succeed in life. It is this belief that led a president and his attorney general (Ronald Reagan and Edwin Meese) to deny that there were any homeless except those who wanted to be. Nothing could be more fitting than that Louis L'Amour should have been President Reagan's favorite writer. In 1984, Reagan's campaign ads sold us the myth that everything in the country was just fine, that it was "morning in America," ignoring the corruption, greed, and law-breaking that we now know were rampant during that administration. If you arrange for our government to aid the Contras, knowing that it is against the law to do so, you do so also knowing that the cowboy in the white hat sometimes has to take the law into his own hands to ensure the triumph of "right." Vigilantism has had a long tradition in this country, even in the White House.

In western movies and novels, government officials—mayors, congressmen, and judges—are almost invariably corrupt, pot-bellied, cigar-smoking, conniving rascals who cannot sit a horse. You always know who the bad guys are—they wear suits. Representative government is always a joke, and democracy seldom works except when the mob is rallied by the heroic individual. In our allegiance to western myth we give thanks for the man on the white horse—a dangerous devotion indeed, as countries throughout Europe and South America can testify. As Americans, we look for the stranger to come out of nowhere, like the Lone Ranger, and bring about "change," our current political slogan.

The survival of the rugged individual as hero (always the "outsider," just as everyone who runs for office nowadays, newcomer or incumbent, claims to be an outsider, a nonpolitician) is testimony to our need to retain our values of hard work, individual initiative, and courage under pressure without actually having to demonstrate these in our own lives. We believe that life, if worthwhile, should be hard, the way it used to be in the old West; but in a technological, urban society, the only cowboys that we have any connection with are those whose voices come to us plaintively over the radio. Movies and TV allow us to experience difficulty vicariously without getting off the couch, without having to breathe dust, get blisters on our bottoms, or get shot at. After watching "Lonesome Dove," we get up out of our chairs exhausted. Surrounded by our families, we have been able to be alone, together, just as we have been able to have a hard life while sitting down.

If we are skeptical of democracy and think of group effort as a Communistic threat or a sign of weakness, if we believe, as we seem to, that every individual can make it on his or her own, and if most individuals in our society believe that either through hard work or through the lottery they will become rich one day, then unions not only are unnecessary, they are hated as interfering with individual rights. And it is rugged individualism that has led to our admiration for that business spin-off from the myth, the entrepreneur, the financial cowboy who is admired for swindling investors, browbeating labor, and exploiting the environment. In business we often seem determined to ignore the achievements of the group, usually the workers, to give false credit to the individual. Although it was the American taxpayers, through their representatives in Congress, who saved Chrysler, we insisted on making Lee Iacocca our hero, and he was happy to accept the honor, as well as a huge salary and bonuses.

I

Wallace Stegner's early experiences taught him the falsity of the myth of individual self-sufficiency and the get-rich-quick mentality that often accompanies it. As a young child he spent some time in an orphanage, when his parents were too poor to take care of him and his brother; and then he went on to spend long summers on the prairie, alone—without his brother (who after the first summer had a job in town) or any friends—while his father tried to homestead a wheat farm in Saskatchewan. He learned early on how it felt to be isolated: "You don't get out of the wind but learn to lean and squint against it. You don't escape sky and sun, but wear them in your eyeballs and on your back. You become acutely aware of yourself. The world is very large, the sky even larger, and you are very small" (*Wolf Willow* 8).

Stegner is probably the only important writer who lived into the 1990s who actually experienced the pioneering period of North American history, on the last unsettled frontier. Something happens to the psyche when one is alone a great deal in such an overwhelmingly large environment. Perhaps a permanent sort of modesty sets in, a sense of helplessness in the face of forces quite beyond the power of human muscle or spirit. In such circumstances we realize that only by helping one another can we be saved from the drought, the blizzard, the distances, and the omnipresent emptiness. Stegner was not only often physically alone but often emotionally cut off as well. His older brother, tough and strong, outshone Stegner, who was smaller, weaker, and often sickly. Stegner's father favored the more athletically inclined brother and often mocked Wallace for his lack of "manhood."[3]

Several of Stegner's short stories reflect the emotional isolation that he felt growing up. "In the Twilight" concerns a young boy, Bruce, who is determined to prove his manliness by remaining stoically unaffected by the sight of his father butchering a sow in preparation for winter. His mother worries about Bruce and his brother watching:

> "I don't think they should see things like that," the mother said helplessly. . . .
> . . . "Oh, rats," he [the father] said. "I always watched butcherings when I was a kid. You want to make them so sissy they can't chop the head off a rooster?" (140)

His mother tells Bruce not to go, but he says, "Ah, heck," determined to be tough and live up to the frontier code, and then deliberately disobeys her. He does not want to be a mama's boy, the worst thing a male can be in a frontier society. But when, after a chase, his father kills the sow, Bruce throws up in front of his father, brother, and friends, and he feels so faint that he has to go into the house to lie down—ashamed. Once again, he fails the test of toughness and is isolated by his failure.

Chided and mocked by his father and older brother, Stegner's fictional counterpart can find comfort only in books and in winning his mother's admiration by succeeding in school. In another story, "The Volunteer," we see this same figure, now called David, caught up in another sort of loneliness. Rather than on the homestead or in the frontier town, this isolation comes in a larger, settled town (presumably Great Falls, Montana, where Stegner moved when he was eleven) because of the father's occupation. Always the rugged individual in these stories, the father is a bootlegger and runs a "blind pig," an illegal bar in his home. Afraid of the law, the family moves frequently, so that David has no friends. At school he works hard to become the teacher's favorite, and at home, if one can call it that, only his mother seems to care for him. Out of his loneliness and frustration he has a sudden realization that suggests an incipient maturity. Dreaming of revenge against his father, who has isolated and mocked him, he suddenly thinks of something besides his own hurt feelings, someone else for a change—his mother:

> Understanding and shame dawned on me together. . . . There was this one person in the entire world who loved me wholly, only this one that I could wholly trust. And if I thought myself lonely, desolate, friendless, abused, what should I think of her? . . . Outside my hateful house I had been able to gather praise with both hands, and bring it back to her and have it doubled. But who praised her? Who helped her? What did she have? (307)

With this step away from himself toward concern for others, David has taken his first step toward what Stegner would define as maturity— not just rejecting his father's male arrogance but taking as his own the qualities expressed by his mother toward him: concern, compassion, and understanding.

Such stories, as well as several autobiographical nonfiction pieces, make it clear that a dichotomy developed early in the author's mind between the intolerant individualism represented by his father and the neighborly tendencies toward caring and cooperation represented by his mother—and it was his mother whom he learned to admire. This dichotomy is made even more graphic in a third story, "Butcher Bird." Here the father, mother, and boy travel the four miles from their the Saskatchewan homestead to welcome their new neighbors, Mr. and Mrs. Garfield, who have come over from England. Mr. Garfield is pleasant and kindly, but his gentle ways irritate the boy's father, Harry, who during the visit becomes increasingly grouchy. The mother and son, however, are charmed by the man's courtesy and hospitality—the couple serve lemonade and play their gramophone (a new experience for the visitors), and Mr. Garfield makes a point of talking to the boy.

In the conflict between the mother's and father's responses to Garfield, there is a subtext of commentary on gender roles in our society. Because Garfield speaks politely, responds to beauty, and is kind and generous, the father thinks of him as a sissy—that is, from the male, ruggedly individualistic point of view Garfield expresses qualities and emotions that the father (and the frontier, masculine society he represents) feels are appropriately expressed only by women. A man should be rough, stoic, and practical. After the visitors leave, the father mocks Garfield's manner of speaking and his dislike of killing things: "'I just can't bear to shoot anything any more,' he said, and laughed" (155). And then a few minutes later, after cleaning the .22 that Garfield gave the boy (making him promise to kill nothing but those animals that kill for the fun of it), he tests the gun by shooting a harmless little sparrow, despite the mother's protests and the boy's horrified response.

The death of the bird suggests the anti-life, anti-loving force of traditional male values. Nothing soft, gentle, harmless, or beautiful should survive. This attitude stands for all the negative qualities in humankind that Stegner would resist. It represents the arrogance that has allowed men to carelessly despoil the land. It represents the greed and competition that invariably lead to cruelty and violence—and, inevitably, war.

Throughout Stegner's work it is womankind that is most likely to represent the best in humanity, and it is certain frontier male values, particularly as distorted by the popular imagination, that represent the worst. The very fact that life-affirming qualities can be expressed by a male, Mr. Garfield, points out that they are not genetic, bound to one sex, but cultural. Males must express their individuality not in uncaring toughness but in resisting peer pressure and role pressure to embrace the best in humankind, to define "manhood" on their own terms. This is the challenge that the boy—Bruce, David, or whatever his name may be in story or novel—must face. "Growing up," gaining maturity, will become a very different matter for him as versus his father.

Distressed by the persistence of the myth of rugged individualism, Stegner sees a society that has not yet grown up. These early stories and *The Big Rock Candy Mountain* reflect a theme out of his own life—the passing of the frontier into a new stage of social development. Bruce Mason, Stegner's counterpart in the novel, arrives in Saskatchewan by horse and wagon but leaves several years later by automobile. But we also see in the novel, and the stories related to it, a resistance to change by many and a clinging to old values (as represented by the father figure) regardless of new circumstances. But beyond reflecting a theme in Stegner's own life, these works also reflect a major theme in American literature of the late nineteenth and early twentieth centuries—the passing away of a rural, primitive society and the growth of an urban, industrial society and the problems of adjusting to that change. We see this theme in *Winesburg, Ohio*, in *Sister Carrie, Main Street, My Ántonia*, and *The Sound and the Fury*, and in dozens of other novels of the period, as well as in such plays as *The Little Foxes, The Glass Menagerie*, and *Death of a Salesman*. Bo Mason, the father figure in Stegner's *The Big Rock Candy Mountain*, was born, as the author says, fifty years too late to strike it rich on the frontier; but with an almost childlike faith in the values passed on to him by family and culture, he cannot give up looking for his big chance. There is sadness in his adherence to mistaken notions, but there is more than sadness, something close to tragedy, in the brutal consequences of his failure. In his condition there is a metaphor for American society as a whole insofar as it tries to relive the past, or deal with the present in inappropriate terms.

Although Stegner gives considerable attention in his work to the maturation of young, semi-autobiographical protagonists such as Bruce Mason, the problem of growing up is not just a matter for the young, as Stegner illustrates in an early novel (one of the few that have gone out of print), *On a Darkling Plain*. In this novel, as in the stories we have just looked at, the conflict is between arrogant, intolerant individualism on the one side and caring, giving cooperation on the other. But this time the conflict is inter-

nal, in the mind and heart of a grown man. Stegner makes use of his childhood experiences on the prairie to describe the life of an isolated individual
who must come to terms with himself, his values, and his role in (or away
from) society. The novel raises the question, Can a human being live happily or successfully without love, companionship, and interaction with or
help from others? Here, as elsewhere, Stegner's answer is No. The best part of
human nature comes out in a concern for, a duty to, others.

The novel can be seen as a modern version of the Robinson Crusoe story
wherein life is reduced to basics, this time on the barren "sea" of the Great
Plains. Edwin Vickers is a Canadian veteran of World War I who has been
wounded, then gassed, and as a result discharged early. His war experiences
have embittered him against all society. He has played his manly part in
war, has gained his medals, and could be considered a hero; but he hates
even thinking about the role he has played, and the violence and brutality
have sickened him not only toward war but toward humankind as a whole.
So although he has money after his discharge from the service and he has a
family in Vancouver, he decides to escape humankind by taking up an abandoned homestead in Saskatchewan, far from the nearest town or even
neighbor.

On his way to his isolated post on the prairie, he stops at the small town
that is two hiking days from his homestead. At the general store where he
buys his provisions, he is barely polite to those he meets in town; he feels an
intolerance even toward the people who mean well and are kindly toward
him. His hostility is broken only by a grudging acceptance of his nearest
neighbors, a farm couple and their daughter—who are inclined to leave him
alone. His first lesson in community comes to him when he finds that he
cannot build a satisfactory home of sod without the help of the farmer and
his horses. The second lesson comes when he finds, through the agency of
the neighbor's daughter, that communicating with some other human being
is essential to his mental and emotional stability. A further lesson is driven
home when he encounters another man living alone out on the prairie—a
wild, dirty scoundrel more animal than human—and learns that isolation
does not necessarily bring nobility of mind or purpose.

Vickers's final transformation into a social animal comes through the
daughter, with whom, as the novel progresses, he falls in love. Her illness and
death in the 1918 flu epidemic at first drive him back into an angry isolation,

but later, after he too is stricken, he is led by her memory to devote himself to helping the community in its crisis. Although he is a grown man who has experienced much—even war, which archetypically is supposed to change boy into man—it takes the example of the love and concern of a woman to pull him out of his childish sense of total independence and into a world where caring for others can justify one's existence.

II

When the Stegner homestead failed from years of unbroken drought, the family moved to Great Falls, Montana, for a few months and then settled in Salt Lake City. Although his childhood in Saskatchewan had not been without its good times, Wallace found true joy in Salt Lake City by joining the Mormon social clubs (although never becoming a Mormon), belonging to a community for the first time. He came to admire the Mormons, in large part because they expressed a spirit so totally opposite to the outlaw, get-rich-quick spirit of his father, a spirit he describes in *The Big Rock Candy Mountain*. Stegner said of Bo Mason, the figure in the novel patterned after his father, that "he would have done very well as a mountain man. Been just as careless, just as reckless, just as wild, just as greedy. Whatever else, the American way was made for him" (Stegner and Etulain 47).

While his father, struggling alone, had failed, the Mormons, working together, had tamed an incredibly forbidding landscape. These polar opposites took root in his mind early in his career, for during the years 1937 to 1942, as he struggled to complete *The Big Rock Candy Mountain*, he stopped to write his history *Mormon Country*. Those opposites are brought together in *Mormon Country* when he writes of the conflicts between the Gentiles and the Mormons, the mining camps and the homesteaders, as well as about some of the desperadoes who brought color to the Utah frontier. Of one such he writes,

Among the legends of the rugged individualists, the anti-social wild men, put down Rafael Lopez, who, in the words of Ma Joad about Pretty Boy Floyd, wasn't a bad boy till they crowded him too hard. He was—or is—the apotheosis of the spirit of the mining camps, an animal with only a varnish of domestication over him. His career throws into strong light the differences between the camps and the Mormon villages in the valleys a few miles from Lopez' last hideout. (*Mormon Country* 279–80)

While Stegner was writing this, he was also writing about Bo Mason, who, like Stegner's father, had gone into the heart of Mormon country to make his living as a bootlegger, a career that was not as flashy as that of Lopez but clearly just as despised by the community (maybe even more so, since it had no false glamour attached to it) and a source of shame for both the young Stegner and his fictional counterpart, Bruce Mason.

Stegner's answer to that archetypal rugged individual, the western bad-man who has been elevated to folk hero and legend, is found in his novel *The Preacher and the Slave* (later called *Joe Hill*). Its protagonist, Joseph Hillstrom, was a Wobbly leader and organizer who was arrested and convicted of murdering a storekeeper during a holdup in Salt Lake City. The IWW accused the government—in a very anti-union state—of railroading Hillstrom, and when he was executed, he become a labor martyr and, shortly, the subject of legend. Stegner bases his "fictional biography" on as much fact as he was able to uncover during his extensive research. But Hill was a mysterious figure and, as such, ripe for mythmakers; Stegner takes the other tack, of debunking the legend. He fills in the blanks, primarily concerning the character's personality and background, by depicting him as a self-absorbed, arrogant loner. According to Stegner's interpretation, Hill was essentially a stick-up man who, using his union activities as a cover and his antagonism for society as a rationalization for his violence, becomes a western mythic hero. A thief, and a not very courageous thief, may remind us strongly of all those many western badmen who have been made the subject of story and song—and Joe Hill certainly had his song.

In Stegner's hands, Joe Hill is not a sympathetic hero. He seems to be motivated essentially by a general antipathy toward anyone in society who has more than he does, who does not believe in the union as he does. Even his belief in the union is questionable, since he scorns most members because they are unwilling to make the complete sacrifices of time and effort that Hill thinks he, himself, makes. Like the gunslinger, he is not so much concerned with social justice—he cares little about other people—as he is bent on having his own way. He is a sociopath, without glamour when one encounters him in the flesh.

The novel is a telling testament against all those qualities that we usually associate with rugged individualism. Stegner uses realism, the exposé of what is behind the romantic veneer, to remind us of what it really is that we glorify when we enshrine such people as martyrs to a cause or make them symbols of a romantic vision of a free and irresponsible way of life.

Stegner worked hard on *The Preacher and the Slave*, not only reading every account available—newspapers, union literature, and trial transcripts—but also interviewing anyone he could find who had known or seen Joseph Hillstrom. He went so far as to retrace Hillstrom's steps through the Utah State Penitentiary yard to face the firing squad. Nevertheless, although the novel is well written and compelling, fraught with the fascination one might have in reading the account of a serial murderer, it was not a success. Stegner was so disappointed by its failure that he gave up writing novels for ten years. There are several possible reasons for the book's failure. First is certainly the lack of suspense here: we know from the beginning that Hill will die at the end. Second is the lack of a hero that the reader can identify with. But third, and perhaps most important, is the possibility that people do not like to have their myths demythologized.

In his introduction to Ben Vorpahl's *My Dear Wister: The Frederic Remington–Owen Wister Letters*, Stegner explores the creation of the cowboy myth:

In [these] pages we watch the complete, triumphant ontogeny of the cowboy hero, the most imagination-catching and durable of our mythic figures. Owen Wister and Frederic Remington, whose collaboration is the subject of Ben Vorpahl's study, create him before our eyes. They begin to mold him out of the observed realities of the brief, furious, passing empire of the cattlemen. They shape him by imitation and trial and error into the hero of a romantic fiction, and in the process they are themselves shaped, as the cowboy image is, by the torque of an anonymous, public, everywhere-and-nowhere myth making impulse. Believing they record reality, they helplessly remake it larger than life, until when they are done their creation rides off the page into the sunset of a thousand horse operas, the free, lonely, self-reliant, skilled, eternally ambiguous embodiment of a national, indeed a human, fantasy. (*One Way 109*)

Stegner points out that there was a third man beyond Wister and Remington who popularized the figure of the cowboy as rugged individual, Theodore Roosevelt. Stegner's comment brings to mind Michael Reynolds's biography of Hemingway, in which he shows how influential Roosevelt was in forming the perceptions of the young Hemingway. It may well be that at bottom the enduring popularity of this author's work, in particular the Hemingway hero, has had something to do with the hero's kinship to the cowboy archetype. Both tend to follow the pattern of the laconic, stoic, self-contained loner; and the chaotic lawlessness of the old West matches rather well Hemingway's "nada," the chaos of World War I in *A Farewell to Arms* or of the Civil War in *For Whom the Bell Tolls*.

The first of Stegner's two cowboy stories reveals Stegner's views of the archetype that grew out of the Wister-Remington-Roosevelt womb. "Genesis" is the fictional part of that history-memoir-story called *Wolf Willow*, nearly everybody's favorite Stegner book. It is a story of the death and destruction visited on the cattle ranches in Stegner's part of Saskatchewan during the terrible winter of 1906–7. It is also the story of survival, the survival of a tenderfoot Englishman, Rusty Cullen, who has joined up to become a ranch hand and who learns that "what would pass for heroics in a softer world was only chores" (450). In a futile effort to round up as many cattle as possible before they freeze, the drovers are caught in a blizzard so fierce that they barely manage to save themselves. They do so only by group effort, by cooperation and sacrifice for others—no one of them could have made it alone. Rusty Cullen's thoughts at the end of his ordeal summarize Stegner's thoughts about the frontier as it really was experienced:

> The Rusty Cullen who sat among them was a different boy, outside and inside, from the one who had set out with them two weeks before. He thought that he knew enough not to want to distinguish himself by heroic deeds: single-handed walks to the North Pole, incredible journeys, rescues, what not. Given his way, he did not think that he would ever want to do anything alone again, not in this country. Even a trip to the privy was something a man might want to take in company. (450)

In *Wolf Willow*, in *Mormon Country*, and in another Mormon history, *The Gathering of Zion*, it is domestication, so often mocked by western romance, that really counts, that is shown to have made the difference between a civilized society and one that lacked order and justice, one that survived and flourished or one that either changed or perished. Western towns died for various reasons, but we are beginning to see the ghost town not as a romantic relic but as a monument to individual greed—the free enterprise system gone berserk, raping and poisoning the earth. In all of these books, one of Stegner's themes is to show just how difficult pioneer life really was, to show hardship, as in the "Ordeal by Handcart" chapter in *The Gathering of Zion*, that was nearly beyond belief, to show a reality that has too often been forgotten, too often been glossed over by a veneer of romance. In the horse opera it is the rugged individual, the lone horseman, who comes to the aid of the community; whereas in life, with few exceptions, it was the community that saved the individual. In the saga of the West as told in romance, it is the rugged individual who pioneers—we have always focused on the adventurers, as Stegner calls them—but in fact it was the family unit that made survival possible and created the real West of farms and ranches.

In the more recent past throughout the West, but particularly in the land of gridlock, bulldozers, and drought that we call California, it was the developer who took on the mantle of the rugged individualist. In the 1980s we heard that the developers, largely in the West and Southwest, along with their savings and loan colleagues were going to cost this generation, and several generations in the future, as much as three hundred billion dollars. Every man, woman, and child in the United States owes at least two thousand dollars to pay for the lifestyles of the rich and famous. At this writing there have been only forty-seven trials—out of a thousand bankruptcies and government takeovers—for fraud and conspiracy in the savings and loan scandal. How do these crooks get away with it? It would seem to be at least in part because they appeal to our basic values, including rugged individualism. When someone like Charles Keating (often photographed wearing a cowboy hat), who alone is costing us three billion dollars, gets on TV and claims he has done nothing wrong and that it is government interference that has caused his problems, a good portion of our population will believe him. But we know that for years the government has approved of this kind of activity. Why else would former president George Bush's son Neil have worked for an outfit called Silverado Savings and Loan. As a country we elected two self-proclaimed cowboys, Reagan and Bush, to the presidency in a row, and that should be enough fantasy for any culture. And, oh, how that wonderful old realist Mark Twain would love it—especially since one of those cowboys was a graduate of Choate and Yale.

Wallace Stegner has created the archetypal developer in Tom Weld in the novel *All the Little Live Things*. Weld is not a bad person, he is just following the American dream. His bulldozers and chainsaws run day and night, cutting down the oaks and eucalyptus, scalping and leveling the green foothills. He thinks of himself as reflecting the pioneer spirit, fighting against the elements and wrestling with nature and government bureaucracy to create civilization. But, typical of the rugged individualist, he has no regard for the earth and no sense of community. By contrast to Weld's unconscious selfishness and carelessness, Stegner provides in the novel, a woman, Marian Catlin, who, like so many women in his novels, is a nurturer, a person closely connected to "all the little live things," always concerned about others, always tolerant of the foibles and mistakes of her neighbors. It is her spirit that Stegner clings to, that can give us some hope for the future. For, as he says in his essay "The Book and the Great Community": "No risk, as Josiah Royce once said, is ever private or individual, and no accomplishment is merely personal. What saves us at any level of human life is union, mutual responsibility, what St. Paul called charity" (*The Sound* 282–83).

If we must name international airports after John Wayne and Ronald Reagan—honoring the myth of rugged individualism as represented in the fictional characters they played (in life and on the screen)—maybe we can grow up enough as a society to look now to a new set of values, perhaps naming something after Mother Teresa. Maybe our "new world order," as declared by former president George Bush, should not reflect the values of Desert Storm so much as it should reflect the values of a woman who has given her life in the service of others, someone who cares deeply about "all the little live things."

CHAPTER THREE

Artist as Environmentalist

Wallace Stegner would seem to have been born with a feeling in his bones for the land around him—alert even in early childhood to its smells, sounds, and sights. By contrast to most of us, who motor on through life, he established relationships with places, sometimes the most god-awful barren places. Always he yearned to know more about any place he might find himself in, but particularly in the West, the region that he considered home. When he came across a place that was unfamiliar to him, he wanted to know its physical history and geological composition, as well as the record of man from the earliest natives to the white explorers to the waves of settlers who stayed or just passed through. The land stimulated his senses, called forth his imagination, and led him to contemplation or wonder. He was a storyteller and seemed to know instinctively that the land had many stories to tell and that any story about people worth telling tied them somehow to their natural environments.

What are the circumstances that might lead someone to become so attached to the land and eventually become an environmental activist? In Wallace Stegner's case we know that the ground was prepared for him by an intimate relationship with nature during childhood. Spending his summers while growing up on the last homestead frontier in Saskatchewan (from 1914 to 1920), he was without playmates, alone with his parents, who through the long days were preoccupied with trying to make the farm function. But rather than suffering from loneliness as one might expect, he found joy in being solitary in nature. He said in looking back, "The bond with the earth that all the footed and winged creatures felt in that country was quite as valid for me" ("Making" 14). Perhaps this reaction is characteristic of all those who eventually become concerned with preserving the natural environment.

From the ages of five to eleven, Wallace found himself on a desolate prairie three to four months a year, a place with "searing wind, scorching sky, tormented and heat-warped light, and not a tree" (*Wolf Willow* 278), a place where livestock could roam for days without encountering the fence of a neighbor. Yet, amazingly enough considering such a barren and hostile environment, Stegner could still look back on a childhood not of suffering and boredom but of "wild freedom, a closeness to earth and weather, a familiarity with both tame and wild animals" (*Wolf Willow* 29). His years on the homestead marked him as a Westerner for life. As he has said, "Expose a child to a particular environment at his susceptible time and he will perceive in the shapes of that environment until he dies" ("Child" 5).

Aside from the empty flatness of the 320 acres of the homestead, its most salient feature was its dryness. There was a source of water—just barely. A short way off the property, near the Montana line, there was coulee where in most seasons water did not really run but rather seeped to the surface and in the spring formed small pools. Wallace and his father would fetch water for the family and livestock from those pools and carry kegs back on their wagon. Wheat was their crop; but it required summer rainfall, and in four years out of five, they were dusted out. During a sixth summer there was so much rain that the wheat was ruined by rust. The family's hopes were dashed, and Wallace's father, who despite his many flaws was a hard worker, gave up in disgust and turned to bootlegging to make a living and after a few months moved the family to Montana. In looking back, the author has said that but for a few inches of rain, his family would have become naturalized citizens and he would have been a Canadian.

That bitter defeat and the missing few inches of rain taught a hard, early lesson that was ingrained in his consciousness and later became a major theme in his environmental writing. Lack of rain or aridity, he repeatedly observed, was the factor that above all defined the West. And lack of water, as well as poor land and inappropriate water laws, became a defining problem for settlers in the West, the determinant of their success or, more often, their failure.[1] Wallace's father's failure to make it as a farmer was a harsh experience for the entire family—even more difficult to accept as time went on because this stint in Saskatchewan would be the only period during which the Stegners were together as a family in a home of their own. But it was not until much later, after Wallace had done the research for his John Wesley Powell biography, that he really understood the basis for that failure and its meaning.

As a child on the prairie, he was painfully aware of more than just the bareness of his surroundings and the weather; he became aware, too, of the animals around him, of "all the little live things," as he would put it in the title of a novel in his later years. He looked upon them with an attitude much like that of the Native American. "The earth was full of animals," he has said about his childhood, "—field mice, ground squirrels, weasels, ferrets, badgers, coyotes, burrowing owls, snakes. I knew them as my little brothers, as fellow creatures, and I have never been able to look upon animals in any other way since" ("Wilderness Letter" 116). With time on his hands, no playmates, and parents deeply engaged in the backbreaking work of carving out a farm in the wilderness, he became far more observant of his surroundings than most children of that age. His senses, which made continuous connection with his surroundings, formed his "internet," his window to the natural world and its drama, as versus the virtual worlds that so entrance our contemporary children.

An important influence leading Wallace to such an early appreciation of nature was a mother who taught him the beauty both of books and of his surroundings, so that the two, literature and the environment, were joined together for him in a positive way in his mother's example early in his life. In addition to the positive influences of his mother was the negative influence of a father who came to stand in Wallace's mind for all the careless, selfish exploiters of nature in the West. His father's relationship to his environment was almost always totally pragmatic. Just as bulbs and fruit trees need both the cold of winter and the returning warmth of spring in order to blossom, so did Wallace need both the hatred for an opportunistic and abusive father and the love for a beauty-seeking and generous mother in order for his environmental conscience to develop. His father could not care less as his mother sought to raise flowers around their little house in the harsh climate of Eastend, and he mocked her when she suggested that they plant trees on the homestead.

An early autobiographical story based on Stegner's childhood on the homestead brings together all three of these elements—the land, mother, and father. "Bugle Song" (also called "Buglesong") is a quiet story, one that creates an atmosphere of solitude through its very quietness. What drama we may find in this story is carried almost subliminally in a subtext of conflict in gender roles involving the boy, although it is a conflict that he is too young to recognize. With only his mother nearby—his father is presumably out working on the homestead—the boy is left to his own devices on the hot and monotonous prairie. We see him first as hard and insensitive to the suffering of animals. He seems to perform his grisly task of trapping gophers and killing them (and on occasion feeding them to his pet weasel) with grim satisfaction as part of the masculine frontier role.

Although absent during the course of the story, it is obviously the father, or his spirit, that dominates this family, and he is the model that the boy feels he should emulate. The mother protests the boy's cruelty and he ignores her, yet he does follow her wishes in preparing for school in the fall by reading his poetry book; and in this and the romantic daydreams generated by the poems, he reflects her softer, more civilized approach to life. Thus, a second conflict in the story, connected to the first but different in kind, is developed between the active, instinctive, and physical on the one hand and the life of the mind—the imagination and the stimulation of the imagination by literature and by nature—on the other.

Both conflicts would persist in Stegner's consciousness throughout his life, and similar contrasts as we see them in "Bugle Song" between male and female roles, between insensitive and sensitive, caring and uncaring, are carried as themes throughout his fiction. We can recognize in these contrasts the conflict at the heart of the western archetype, and the adult Stegner, who plumps down squarely on the side of the mother, becomes a writer who spends much of his career refuting the mythic West and our rationale for exploitation in the doctrine of rugged individualism. This refutation in turn would lead him to such environmental activities as refuting the arguments of the Sagebrush Rebellion—which involved western landowners and developers, and the politicians whom they controlled, who wanted the federal government to "return" federal land to the states. That land, Stegner pointed out repeatedly in several essays, was never owned by the states.[2]

In his childhood, often alone on the prairie or isolated in his house in town during the harsh winters, Wallace Stegner became an omnivorous reader, and as a small and weak boy, he found that his only successes came by achievement in school. One might have predicted that he, out of such a background, would become a writer, but he never thought of it as even a possibility. Nevertheless, following a long, circuitous route, as described in his essay "Literary by Accident," he eventually became by his late twenties both writer and teacher of writing. His first major success came with *The Big Rock Candy Mountain* (1943), the story of his own growing up and the conflict between the values of his father and those of his mother. In depicting his father as exploiter and his mother as conserver, the novel is an early reflection of the author's evolving environmental conscience.

But the work that really established him as a writer of environmental literature was his biography of John Wesley Powell, *Beyond the Hundredth Meridian* (1954). It brought Powell to the public mind as an early hero in the conservation struggle and brought to the fore the history of the mistakes and controversies of western land and water policy. In reminding us of Powell's assertion, which so infuriated his politician-booster contemporaries, that most of the West beyond the one hundredth meridian was either desert or near desert and that settlement and development must take this into account, Stegner's book can take its place alongside such seminal conservation works as Rachael Carson's *Silent Spring*. In the West, water meant survival, not only for people but for the land itself and all its creatures.

Although embracing Powell's values, Stegner wrote the book not out of a passion for environmentalism but as a tribute to a man he admired. He got onto Powell because his doctoral advisor at the University of Iowa had suggested he write his dissertation on a colleague of Powell's, Clarence Edward Dutton, a nineteenth-century scientist, civil engineer, and literary naturalist. Just by chance, the Stegner family had a cabin on the Fishlake Plateau, right in the middle of the high plateaus that were Dutton's territory. Wallace realized, "all of a sudden history crossed my trail. I found that when I went up Seven Mile I found I knew what had happened there sixty, seventy years before" ("Literary" 12). The literary and the natural environments once again came together in his life.

Although the groundwork had been laid, from childhood to maturity, Wallace Stegner the environmental activist did not emerge until midlife, in the early 1950s, after he had written many short stories and novels and after the research for the Powell biography was nearly finished. Just researching and writing the Powell book taught him a great deal, not only giving him detailed knowledge of the fight for conservation in the West but also providing a different mind-set, a realization of how important and ongoing the battle had been and still was. In addition to his work on Powell, Wallace remained connected to the land, as an inveterate traveler and camper throughout the West, aware of its natural and historical values; but it took a moment, a moment of transformation, to take him from sympathizer to activist.

To trace the history of that moment, we need to go briefly to Stegner's teaching career, which began at a small Lutheran college in Illinois while he was a doctoral student and continued, after his degree, at the University of Utah and then at the University of Wisconsin. He found he had no chance, during the depths of the Depression, to get promoted and gain tenure at either of those universities, so from Wisconsin he went on to Harvard as a Briggs-Copeland Fellow. At Harvard he met a number of famous literary figures, and particularly important to him, as I have said, were Robert Frost and Bernard DeVoto. They became mentors—Frost in literature and DeVoto in conservation, and both in regard to humankind's relations to nature.

Readers have noticed how often Stegner in his fiction quotes Frost, and it could be said that Frost provided a background of metaphor that Stegner adopted and brought into his own talent for figurative language to deal with nature in literary terms. Both Frost and Stegner were basically realists: in the poetry of the one and the fiction of the other, life can be hard; and nature, while it can be beautiful, can also be unforgiving. While nature and a consciousness of nature dominate the work of both men, neither writer ever treats it sentimentally.

But it was DeVoto who would provide the moment of transition for Stegner. They became close friends in Cambridge and had a lot in common, since both had come out of the West to the East and both were non-Mormons from Utah.[3] Both were involved in writing both fiction and history. During the 1940s and 1950s, DeVoto's was one of the few voices in the mainstream media advocating the preservation of public lands and supporting the National Park Service (he had a bully pulpit in his *The Easy Chair* column for *Harper's*). The two men played tennis and badminton together, and Stegner and his wife, Mary, were regulars at DeVoto's Sunday evening martini gettogethers with Harvard luminaries. DeVoto was vociferous and argumentative in support of his convictions, and over the years that Stegner was at Harvard (1939–45), he got an earful of DeVoto's passion for conservation.

Stegner left Harvard after World War II to go to Stanford to found its creative writing program. In 1952 he took a trip around the Colorado Plateau and Grand Canyon areas of the West to do research for the Powell biography and came back fuming over the complaining he had heard throughout the region about the Bureau of Land Management and the National Park Service. Many of the complaints were unjustified and founded on false information, such as the supposition, once again, that the federal government had taken public lands away from the states. He and DeVoto had been corresponding regularly about his research for the Powell book, and in a phone conversation on his return from his trip, Stegner revealed his anger about the attacks on federal land management, which in his view were motivated by greed. If public lands were handed over to the states, then the lumber, mining, and cattle industries would have a much easier time influencing local officials in order to adopt the lands for their own uses and an easier time ignoring the larger public interest.

DeVoto listened impatiently and then told him, "For God's sake, man, don't tell me. I know all about it. You need to sit down and write about it, get the article published, and spread the word."[4] And Stegner did. That was the moment an activist was born. That first article was "One-Fourth of a Nation: Public Lands and Itching Fingers," and he had a difficult time finding a magazine that would publish it. Finally his agents got it placed with *Reporter* magazine for the May 12, 1953, issue.

Wallace Stegner went on to write some sixty articles devoted partially or entirely to conservation, preservation, and environmental problems. These had various subjects and venues. Following his initial *Reporter* article in 1953, he published a piece in the *New Republic* in 1954 called "Battle for the Wilderness" and another in 1955 for *Sports Illustrated* called "We Are Destroying Our National Parks." Probably his most common topic was the aridity of most of the West, which was misunderstood or simply denied, and the multitude of problems that resulted from it. But he also wrote several articles each about the need to preserve our national parks (chronically underfunded), the need to set aside wilderness areas as defined by law, and the need to keep public lands in the hands of the federal government. Other subjects included overpopulation, pollution, rugged individualism, the history of the environmental movement, and the history of public lands and land law. He also wrote essays about various key figures of the movement, including Ansel Adams, Aldo Leopold, Henry David Thoreau, and Bernard DeVoto.

He published these works in diverse magazines, ranging from *Saturday Review, Holiday, American Heritage, Esquire, Westways,* and *Atlantic* to *Smithsonian, Living Wilderness, Wilderness,* and *Sierra Club Bulletin.* These last few he tended to avoid as preaching to the converted, although one of his best essays, a history of the environmental movement in the United States called "It All Began with Conservation" appeared in *Smithsonian.* As pointed out earlier, mainstream publications tended to avoid these kinds of articles, perhaps as too specialized in interest, too editorializing, or too doctrinaire. However, Stegner had the advantage of being a well-known author of fiction and nonfiction whose work, regardless of subject, required editorial attention, if not always acceptance; and his agents worked hard to place his environmental essays in magazines where they would likely do the most good.

Furthermore, one of Stegner's favorite genres was the travel article (which he used to finance his and his wife's travel), and in many of these articles he was able to slip in bits of advocacy or pieces of information that implied conservation. For example, he did an article titled "Lake Powell" for *Holiday,* which, although doing justice to the beauties and advantages of the lake, clearly mourns the loss of Glen Canyon due to the Glen Canyon Dam at Page, Arizona.

Probably Stegner's best-known and most often reprinted piece of environmental writing has been his "Wilderness Letter" (1961).[5] He was asked by David Pesonen to help strengthen his argument for the preservation of wilderness areas in a report Pesonen was preparing for the Outdoor Recreation Resources Review Commission. Stegner's son, Page, has said that his father in reply

> wrote what is now known by every environmentally conscious soul on the planet as the "Wilderness Letter," an argument for the restorative value of wilderness that like Aldo Leopold's "The Land Ethic" and Henry David Thoreau's "Walking" has become one of the central documents of the conservation movement. (*Marking* 110)

The letter is amazing—so beautifully written—yet it was never intended to be published. Stegner brought every tool of his trade as artist to his task, and nearly every sentence of its six printed pages is memorable. The arguments against preserving land as wilderness depended on the idea that in such areas resources would be "locked up" (a potent argument against wilderness during World War II) and that such areas should be opened up for multiple uses, that is, not only for development—roads, houses, mining, lumbering, grazing—but for public recreation—resorts and boating, skiing, bus touring, golfing. Designated wilderness areas would be off limits to nearly everyone except backpackers. What Stegner starts out by saying is that although the letter is a recreation report, he is not going to address possible wilderness uses but the value of the wilderness *idea*. Having wilderness there, simply there, is good for our spiritual health. "We . . . need that wild country available to us, even if we never do more than drive to its edge and look in. For it can be a means of reassuring ourselves of our sanity as creatures, a part of the geography of hope" ("Wilderness" 112, 117).

The letter came into the hands of Stewart Udall, who at the time, 1961, was the secretary of the interior. He was so impressed by it that he set aside his own speech for a wilderness conference and instead simply read aloud Stegner's letter. The letter came to be published several times and ended up as a sort of anthem of preservation that spread around the world.

In 1961, several months before the letter was composed, Udall had appointed a reluctant Stegner as an assistant to the secretary of the interior and had given him as his first job the task of surveying and reporting on a number of areas that were being considered for designation as national parks. Stegner served for four months, and his last few weeks were spent in the Library of Congress doing research and preparing an outline for a book by Udall. Stegner had suggested the project, and he suggested various possibilities for development and wrote a sample chapter for what became *The Quiet Crisis.*[6] Even in his role as assistant to the secretary of the interior, he was able to bring his art to bear on his concern for preservation.

In addition to his many articles, Wallace celebrated his friend Bernard DeVoto's contributions to the struggle by writing his biography, *The Uneasy Chair* (1974), and editing his letters. He edited *This Is Dinosaur: Echo Park and Its Magic Rivers* (1955), which was largely responsible for preventing the construction of the Echo Park dam, and with his son, Page, wrote about our complex and generally destructive relationship with our continent in

American Places (1981). Then in 1987 he published *The American West as Living Space*, a collection of lectures, given at the University of Michigan, that were largely concerned with the problems of conservation.[7]

But beyond even these things, in a final triumph of his art as an expression of his beliefs, he was able bring together the two strands of his life, his devotion to the writing of fiction and his devotion to the preservation of the environment. He once told Ansel Adams, the famed landscape photographer with whom he served on the Sierra Club board of directors and whom he greatly admired, "I do wish I was able to bring my art [referring here to his novels and short stories] and my advocacy for conservation together as successfully as you have."[8] But he did—more subtly, perhaps, but that combination is still there. We find it in many of the stories and in nearly every novel he wrote, most explicitly in *A Shooting Star*, written midcareer (1961), and in his last novel, *Crossing to Safety*, in 1987. And what was extremely important to him was that he accomplished this task without perverting his fiction by making it a vehicle for overtly preaching a message.

However, even long before that turning point when he became an activist, his fiction often revealed the values and attitudes that became the foundation for his environmental activities. Looking back on his very first novel, *On a Darkling Plain* (1940), we can see that he exposes the myth of rugged individualism as the basis for the settlement of the West and endorses the importance of social cooperation. In *The Big Rock Candy Mountain* (1943) he tackles the American Dream, finding it far more damaging than does Dreiser in *An American Tragedy* or Fitzgerald in *The Great Gatsby*. Almost alone among major writers of our time, he realized that the dream has not only twisted our lives and corroded our values but also despoiled the very land that has given us such hope. And that hope, as represented by the frontier, is what gave the West such a symbolic role in representing the dream and has made the perpetuation of the mythic West possible.

Eight years after publishing his first activist article in 1953, Stegner published his fifth novel, *A Shooting Star*. In it, the heroine's brother, for no apparent reason other than greed (although he seems to have plenty of money), wants to take the family land and convert it to an upscale housing development, whereas the heroine, Sabrina, wants to donate it for a park. And the developer as a villain of sorts appears once again in *All the Little Live Things* (1967), but this time as a buffoon who has no idea what his bulldozers

are doing to the green foothills. The novel, perhaps the most environmentally conscious of all Stegner's fictions, concerns the value of life, of all life,
when it is left naturally to flourish without our attempts to dominate it with
our chemicals and machines.

His Pulitzer Prize–winning novel, *Angle of Repose* (1971), takes him back
to Dutton, Powell, and another colleague of Powell's, Clarence King, and the
days of the Geological Survey in the 1870s. The fictional Oliver Ward, patterned after another real participant in the survey, is a civil engineer whose
grand project is to build an irrigation canal in Idaho to bring water to the
high desert. Partly because of the difficulty and expense of creating the canal
and partly due to his integrity, which will not allow him to mislead his
investors, Ward fails. In all of this, Stegner is telling the archetypal story of
Easterners who come to the West to make their fortune, but with that story
there is a subtext about the lack of water in the West, a dramatization of the
doctrine right out of John Wesley Powell's *Report on the Lands of the Arid
Region of the United States* (1878).

Stegner thought of himself as essentially a novelist, and although he
wrote many different kinds of things—history, biography, travel articles, literary criticism, and short stories—writing novels was, he felt, his vocation.
He was an ambitious man—it was through his novels that he felt that he
would make a reputation. But after the initial article prompted by DeVoto
and subsequent service on the National Parks Advisory Board and the
boards of the Sierra Club and Wilderness Society, he felt a deep obligation to
write in service of his environmental convictions as often as he could make
time for. It was David Brower, the director of the Sierra Club, who talked
him into editing *This Is Dinosaur*. The book was so successful in marshaling
public opinion and convincing Congress to abandon the Echo Park dam
that Brower was continually after Stegner to write more. "He had," Brower
would say admiringly, "a way with words."[9] But Stegner was first and foremost a novelist, and Brower hit a nerve when he called one time to talk him
into another project, telling him that he was wasting his time on mere "stories" when the fate of the world hung in the balance. Stegner's anger was
partly in response to Brower's apparent contempt for the art of creative writing, but it also, no doubt, was prompted in part by guilt.

Wallace Stegner was a man with an active conscience. While he would make a number of significant contributions to the cause throughout the latter part of his career, including the famous "Wilderness Letter," he was torn on the one side by the feeling that he could do more and on the other by his devotion to the art of fiction. He reflected that internal conflict in a letter to the Wilderness Society's Tom Watkins, who was preparing an article about Stegner's environmental contributions:

> I have not been an effective or even eager activist. In all the issues that matter, there are dozens of people—David Brower, Ed Wayburn, Howard Zahniser, the hard nosed, tough, and durable types . . . —who have had an immediate, practical, effective usefulness. I never have. . . . Actually I would like, and would always have liked, nothing better than to stay home and write novels and histories. . . . I am a paper tiger, Watkins, typewritten on both sides. Get that in somewhere. (Watkins 100)

Typewritten, yes, but a voice, nevertheless, that will persist in our culture, not only in several dozen essays but in a dozen novels, most of which are still in print. Near the end of his novel *All the Little Live Things*, bringing to bear his literary skill to define our place in nature in one of his most poignant passages, he has the dying Marian tell the grief-stricken Joe Allston:

> Don't feel bad. I'm glad you love me, but I hope you and Ruth won't grieve. It's right there should be death in the world, it's as natural as being born. We're all part of a big life pool, and we owe the world the space we fill and the chemicals we're made of. Once we admit it's not an abstraction, but something we do personally owe, it shouldn't be hard. (287)

Wallace Stegner was not just a Pulitzer Prize– and National Book Award–winning novelist, he was an artist with a conscience, an artist with important ideas for our time about humankind and our relations to the land around us. That he had such a variety of weapons in his arsenal—as accomplished writer of fiction and nonfiction, as historian, as active outdoorsman, as amateur naturalist and geologist, and as teacher—made him almost unique in the pantheon of environmental heroes. Just stop for a moment to think how his role as teacher of writing during his twenty-five years at Stanford connected with his environmentalism; look at the many students of his who have been connected with the land and with a strong sense of place:

Larry McMurtry in Texas, Wendell Berry in Kentucky, Edward Abbey in New Mexico and the Southwest, Ken Kesey in Oregon, James Houston in California, and Ernest Gaines in Louisiana.

Other writers have made their reputations by shocking us, by rebelling, by engaging in suicidal excesses, by scoffing at every positive element in American life. Stegner never took the cheap path to fame. Certainly, he himself was not above harsh criticism of certain behaviors or attitudes in his society. But he was an artist wherein the man and his work were of one piece constructed on the bedrock of integrity. The secret of Wallace Stegner is that he never felt sorry for himself, never indulged himself at the expense of others, but cared deeply for those around him, for his country, its land and its people.

CHAPTER FOUR

Evaluating the Environmentalist

The story of Wallace Stegner's participation in the conservation movement would not be complete without a few words about how he has been viewed by the environmentalist community. The increasing internal politicization of the movement in recent years has fragmented it into groups that are often in conflict both in their philosophies and in the ways they are willing to act. In discussing this, we get into a complex world where differences have been drawn between preservationist, conservationist, ecologist, environmentalist, and ecoterrorist, and where, from the point of view of many, the degree of commitment to activism, even violence, can provide a person's credentials. Since they overlap to some extent, all of the labels above except ecoterrorist could be applied to Stegner; however, always a moderate, even in support of his deepest convictions, Stegner has not always been admired and indeed has been, by some, scorned.

One of two articles that analyze the history of Stegner's environmental philosophy and activity and evaluate them in some detail is "Stegner and Stewardship" by Ann Ronald. Well known for her extensive writing about Edward Abbey, she does express limited admiration for what Stegner accomplished but admires him much less than she does Abbey. Abbey, of course, is best known for his novel *The Monkey Wrench Gang*, the story, in Ronald's words, of "a merry band of ecological anarchists" ("Edward Abbey" 607). There is a Wild West romanticism in the band's raids on trucks, tractors, trains, and bridges, as if their progress through Arizona and Utah was patterned after that of the James gang. The band expresses that rugged individualism and anarchism that Stegner despised.

In another essay that surveys and evaluates Stegner's environmental record, "Wallace Stegner and the Environmental Ethic: Environmentalism as a Rejection of Western Myth," Brett J. Olsen also brings up Edward Abbey for comparison. He points out that Abbey's

> arguments for defiant ecoterrorism, as well as those of his heirs in the ecodefense movement, reflected the same exaggerated sense of "cowboy" individualism prevalent among nineteenth-century vigilantes, modern day cowboys, and "Sagebrush Rebels" [those congressmen and senators who demanded that the federal government "give back" its lands to the states]. (137)

 Olsen sees Abbey as victim of a frontier romanticism, a frontier that as an Easterner come lately to the West he, unlike Stegner, never experienced firsthand. Contrary to Abbey's, Stegner's philosophy can be described by the key word "realism."

Since no one is seriously physically hurt by the activities of the Monkey Wrench Gang, one can take Abbey's novel as hyperbolic metaphor. And as metaphor, Stegner would agree with it as an argument and with many of its ultimate goals but would disagree with it as a model for actual behavior. One need only go back to his history: although he was opposed to the Vietnam War and even marched in demonstrations against it, he was equally opposed to the demolition of the Stanford campus by rampaging young demonstrators. He did not like the self-righteousness, the carelessness, the antihistoricism, and the total rejection of all authority he observed in many of his students of the late 1960s and early 1970s.

He had come up the hard way out of poverty and from a family that lived as outlaws, with a mother and father who never went beyond the eighth grade. He had earned his position in life, and he resented those—largely ignorant (and proud of it) and often privileged—who would muffle him and deny him his accomplishments. There is a certain ironic parallel here with the elitism and know-nothingism of the urban environmentalist radical, who has no knowledge of the history of environmentalism in this country, who has never gotten his or her hands dirty, and who wants to tell country people barely making a subsistence living how treat the land.

It is significant, then, to note in evaluating their respective approaches that Stegner and Abbey were of different generations. Stegner was of a generation that valued restraint and respect for the opinions of others and that hoped to convince others through dialogue to reach a consensus; Abbey was of a generation impatient with politeness and politics, one that demanded confrontation. There is some irony in the fact that Abbey was one of Stegner's students at Stanford and was influenced to some degree by his environmentalist consciousness, and some irony as well in the fact that Stegner, no matter how much he may have disagreed with some of Abbey's ideas, praised his contributions to environmentalism when he died.

Another example illustrates the differences between them. On a trip to the Southwest just after World War II, Stegner stopped to admire Hoover Dam. It was an incredible engineering feat. Two decades later, Abbey played with the idea of blowing up such structures. By that time, however, Stegner had changed his mind about dams and regretted particularly the covering over of Glen Canyon, the beauties of which he had explored by boat years before. He had fought against that dam but always felt he had not done enough to convince those, like David Brower of the Sierra Club, who might have had the political will and means to stop it. In his remorse Stegner became a major spokesman for the opposition to several dam projects, including those across the Green River and across the Colorado at the Grand Canyon.

That Stegner changed his mind over the years about a number of things related to environmentalism bothers Ronald. She represents that part of the movement that admires much in the Stegner legacy but is dismayed by his lack of certainty, his apparent lack of passion, and his willingness to, if necessary, compromise (Ronald has stated that in dealing with the dilemma of humankind's relations with the land in the West, "Compromise has rarely been effective" ["Edward Abbey" 604]. One might counter that in a democracy everything is done by compromise.) Stegner showed remorse and frequently admitted guilt as he discovered a more responsible set of values—regretting his bloodthirsty killing of small animals on the homestead, for example, or his admiration for the builders of dams. As Brett J. Olsen has said, "His ready admission of guilt sets him apart from the self-righteous stance assumed by many other environmentalists over the last three decades" (127).

To oversimplify the difference between Abbey and Stegner, one could say that Abbey is the lone cowboy and Stegner the farmer who depends on his neighbors. Throughout the mythic West, the one has been romanticized and the other, if not despised, certainly looked down upon. What young boy would want to give up his six-shooter to be a clod buster with a shovel? Out of his own past on the frontier where he, himself, as a youngster was caught up in the cowboy myth and values, Stegner came to reject its glorification of the lone horseman or mountain man in favor of group action and cooperation, which he began to realize were the actual basis not only for successful settlement but for one's very survival in the frontier West.

Stegner was a realist and a democrat—both large "D" and small. He was a realist not only in his approach to fiction but also in his approach to saving the environment. Abbey can tear down signs and dream of blowing up dams, and others, like Gary Snyder, can meditate in front of an imposing redwood tree. But it took people like Stegner who had the patience to endure hours of meetings (and he hated meetings) of the boards for the National Parks Commission, the Sierra Club, the Wilderness Society, and the Committee for Green Foothills—dreary work that helped to establish national and local parks and the principle of wilderness preservation.

For just this kind of courage, one of the people that Stegner most admired was Howard Zahniser, executive secretary of the Wilderness Society. Zahniser drafted the wilderness bill and over a period of eight years had to revise it more than sixty-six times before it was passed by Congress. Hard work, patience, persistence, and persuasion were, for Stegner, the keys to change hearts and votes in order to change the laws. And changing the laws, he discovered, was crucial—there was no other way to make a significant difference in accomplishing the goals of saving and improving the natural environment.

As I pointed out in the previous essay, it was Bernard DeVoto who took Stegner's conservationist instincts and converted them to activism. And DeVoto's crusade was essentially one that put the federal government up as protector of our western land's heritage against the forces of greedy exploitation. The government was all we the people had to counterbalance the influence of wealth, even though DeVoto felt that the government and its agencies could certainly do a better job of protection. He and Stegner both admired the National Park Service and all that it did despite opposition and lack of resources, but they admired less the National Forest Service and the Bureau of Land Management. These last two were often, in their view, too heavily influenced by the lumber, mining, and cattle industries. But if not the federal government, then who would rein in corporations and rural state legislatures controlled by wealthy constituents?

Stegner's faith in government, as cautious as it might have become, came first out of his frontier background where cooperation was essential for survival. This background provided the basis for his concern for community, consensus, and grassroots democracy. He not only opposed the myth of rugged individualism, on the one hand, but also, on the other, was a booster for many years of the cooperative movement in this country (a movement labeled as "communist inspired" during the 1940s and 1950s by members of Congress and industry trade groups). He wrote more than a dozen essays trying to promote the movement that he felt could, among other things, build communities of interest and provide buying power to the ordinary citizen of moderate means. The movement was for him a demonstration of democracy, of power to the people. A key word connected with Stegner's hopeful dependence on the federal government is "democracy"—he believed in it.

But Ann Ronald, along with Abbey, would seem to have little liking for the government, and she appears to reproach Stegner when she says,

> Stegner suggests a partial reliance on the federal government. In this respect he differs quite radically from a number of his fellow conservationists, because he genuinely believes that proper governmental intervention is a viable course of action. History may have proved otherwise. ("Stegner" 99)

If not the federal government and the legislation to establish the national parks, the Clean Water Act, the Clean Air Act, the Wilderness Act, the Endangered Species Act, the old-growth protection agreement in California, as well as local trash-recycling ordinances—then what? Spiking trees and burning down buildings? This suspicion of government, while not nearly that extreme on Ronald's part, is nevertheless reminiscent of the rhetoric of the Aryan Nation, the survivalists, and others who constantly speak of Ruby Ridge and Waco. It is a corrosive distrust that seems to be endemic to the rural West and South and connected to the mythic ideal of cowboy independence. (Remember that the Virginian, the archetypal "lone cowboy," came from the South and brought its values and rituals with him.) Who hates the federal government more, the logger, miner, or cattle rancher whose living has been taken away by the Endangered Species Act or the radical environmentalist who feels strongly that the government never goes far enough?

There is a basic problem here that gets at the root of our society. Are we willing to accept the will of the people, even when we feel that that will is wrong, and thus, no matter how reluctantly, endorse our form of government? Do we work to change minds through persuasion and argument? Or are we, in the name of the environment or any cause however worthy, going to act against the will of the majority and follow a road similar to that of the radical "pro-lifers," who have decided it is just fine to shoot doctors, burn down clinics, and intimidate patients?

Of course, again, I do not suggest here that Ronald endorses violence. What she does admire is Abbey's total commitment, expressed however that may be, in his art. But distrust of the government, which seems to be so characteristically American, which has been on occasion perfectly justified, and which on the positive side has helped us preserve our independence, can easily mutate into that kind of poisonous, undiscriminating hatred that led to the Oklahoma City bombing. For Stegner, independence, to the degree that it also takes into account the welfare of others, is fine, to be valued.

In an essay called "Variations on a Theme by Crèvecoeur," Stegner contrasts two kinds of independent types in American society as Crèvecoeur described them almost two hundred years ago. The pioneer farmer on the one hand and the wild man on the other. "The farmer's very virtues as responsible husband, father, and home builder are against him as a figure of imagination," Stegner tells us. Whereas, he continues,

> It was Crèvecoeur's wild man, the borderer emancipated into total freedom, first in eastern forests and then in the plains and mountains of the West, who really fired our imaginations, and still does. We have sanitized him somewhat, but our principal folk hero, in all his shapes, good and bad, is essentially antisocial. . . .

Lawlessness, like wildness, is attractive, and we conceive the last remaining home of both to be the West. (106–7)

As Stegner goes on to point out, the attraction of lawlessness did not die with the frontier, or later on with Billy the Kid and Butch Cassidy, but continues to the present day. We have repeatedly made heroes out of cold-blooded killers, romanticizing and sanitizing their exploits. Stegner cites the case of Claude Dallas, who, a number of years ago, killed two Idaho game wardens after they had caught him poaching. Rather than paying a small fine, Dallas dry-gulched the wardens and then, as they lay wounded, put bullets in the backs of their heads. This cold-blooded execution hardly carried on the chivalric tradition of the walk-down out of *The Virginian* and a hundred other western movies. For months Dallas escaped capture, partly because of his own survivalist competence but also because he was supplied and protected by people all over the area. They despised the government and forces of law and order more than they were repelled by murder, even senseless, brutal murder. And they admired his self-reliance and his frontier skills. Like Stegner's own father, Dallas had frontier skills but no frontier to go to except the frontier of lawlessness ("Variations on a Theme by Crèvecoeur" 107).

Dallas is not the only prominent example. At this writing, Eric Rudolph, who is thought to have bombed the Atlanta Olympics and at a least one abortion clinic, is still on the loose. He has depended on his survivalist skills, as did Dallas, and like Dallas has received help from friends and neighbors so that he has been able to hide out in the woods of North Carolina for more than a year. Notice that he carried out a bombing, one of the most cowardly activities that anyone with a cause can engage in. In the decades to come, will he be celebrated like Billy the Kid? Some of Edward Abbey's anarchist protagonists, self-righteously taking the law into their own hands, are at times awfully close to the "wild man" type and certainly replicate the lone cowboy myth. Which do we have here, the Lone Ranger or Billy the Kid? And what about the Unibomber, who hid out in the deep woods, lived a primitive existence, and attacked the technology that so many environmentalists would destroy or outlaw? While Stegner advocates individual action to benefit the environment, he, as always, looks primarily to cooperation and consensus of community—a far less glamorous, exciting, and engaging alternative.

Ronald chides Stegner for admiring the yeoman American farmer as idealized by Crèvecoeur and Thomas Jefferson, apparently missing Stegner's point of the comparison of types ("Stegner" 98). It is the single-family farmer, a reality (up to now) rather than a myth, that Stegner admires, as versus the wild man, the outlaw, the mountain man, the lone cowboy; for it is this farmer who has built, helped his community, and stuck to the land and improved it. He is not the exploiter, the ruthless seeker of riches, the glamorized outlaw. Stegner may, as Ronald charges, romanticize the farmer, but it is hard to see that Stegner's efforts in that regard could ever compare to the glamorization of the "wild man" throughout our history. After all, the yeoman farmer does the dull thing, the hard thing, and makes the best of what he has.

It is certain that this distinction between clodhopper and lone cowboy came to Stegner's consciousness out of his own frontier experience, before he found these types labeled in a somewhat different way by Crèvecoeur. Stegner, himself, in earlier writings (*The Big Rock Candy Mountain*), had come up with a similar distinction, that between "sticker" and "boomer," contrasting types on the frontier that matched the personalities of his parents. His father was a boomer, a man born with frontier skills but too late for the frontier, and his mother was a sticker, a woman who wanted nothing more than to be a farmer's wife and have her own home. Those who have had little real contact with an outlaw might forgive Stegner's obvious distaste for the figure in legend since his father *was* one and his family suffered dearly for it. As I suggested in the previous essay, it was the hatred of his exploiter father and love of his conserver mother that may well be thought of as the basis for Stegner's environmentalism.

Beyond his childhood on the frontier, a second influence that led Stegner to have some faith in government was his experience of researching and writing his book about John Wesley Powell (*Beyond the Hundredth Meridian*). The one influence really led to the other. In speaking of his homestead experience, Stegner has said, "One who has lived the dream, the temporary fulfillment, and the disappointment has had the full course" (*Wolf Willow* 282). In her essay, Ronald points out that "the boy who lived both the dream and the disappointment never forgot the lessons of his youth. So when he went on to become the man who studied John Wesley Powell, Stegner was ready to espouse the truths spoken by a historical figure whose ideas coincided with his own" ("Stegner" 90).

Powell was a major in the Union army and lost his arm at Shiloh. Largely self-educated, he represented the same kind of homespun striving toward achievement in the near-frontier society of Illinois that characterized Lincoln's early career. He was a demonstration of the promise of our democracy—opportunity—and like Lincoln became a champion of democracy. He came out of impoverished circumstances and, with some formal education and more self-education, became a scientist and civil engineer and went on to extraordinary achievements in both science and engineering.

He showed enormous courage not only in his expedition, where he led the party that was first by boat down the Colorado River, but also in fighting Congress, and the special interests that controlled it, as head of the Geological Survey in order to establish a rational lands policy. Stegner admired him for a number of reasons, but particularly for two. First, Powell was, like Stegner, a myth buster, a realist. Stegner's family had been taken in by the dream, the myth of the Garden West propagated by developers and politician partners who proclaimed that "rain followed the plow." In fact the Stegners worked like hell for six years on their homestead and, as we have seen, were dusted out five out of those six. It was Powell who dared state the reality: that most of the West beyond the hundredth meridian was desert or near desert and that very few parts of it got the twenty inches of rain needed to support field crops without irrigation. Powell worked out a scientific way of parceling out homestead lands by use and by availability of water, but Congress rejected his plan.

A second major reason for Stegner's admiration, connected to the first, was that Powell was a scientist in service of the people. He cared little for reward or fame and instead cared for the welfare of his country and its ordinary citizens. He was a democrat, a public servant, and a searcher for useful knowledge. Perhaps his greatest accomplishment was to democratize science. Up to his time, scientific inquiry was totally the province of elitist, wealthy individuals. Science was divided up into fiefdoms that were protected and disputed. Powell fought that monopoly and worked to bring science into government, to open it up, so that talented people, regardless of class or affiliation with elite clubs or universities, could work for discovery with the backing of federal government resources. And although he lost many battles, this one, through courage and perseverance over the course of many years, was won.

Powell felt that government science was essential to our form of government and prerequisite to our cultural advancement and physical well-being.

It was his leadership and the battles he fought for the common man that enabled the government over succeeding years to establish agency after agency in the pursuit of scientific knowledge about the land, its history, its health, the environment, and the nature of nature. This victory, although it has had little recognition even by scientists themselves, is perhaps one of the most significant in the history of the Republic.

It is this sense of science in the service of the ordinary American, Powell's sense, that Stegner embraced as a good. Ronald in her essay quotes Stegner as calling for "a land ethic that unites science, religion, and human feeling." Ronald goes on to comment,

> While such phrases underscore Stegner's prevailing commitment to the ethics of conservation, the latter quotation includes a curious anomaly. The word *science* sounds strangely out of place—naming something closely akin to technology, something many conservationists would blame rather than embrace. ("Stegner" 91)

Ronald is probably right in her assessment. Some conservationists no doubt do feel that way, but this antipathy to science in general is another manifestation of Luddite insanity. If science means the effort to discover the truths of the physical world, then it would seem logical that science must be an integral part of any effort to rationally conserve and preserve the natural environment. And that effort may, horrors of horrors, have to depend in some degree on technology. We will have to solve some of our environmental problems by giving up technology or modifying it radically, but others will have to await technological solutions. Realistically, to speak for Stegner here, it is too late to go back to hunting and gathering.

Stegner's realism leads to an environmental position that Ronald (as well as Stegner himself) labels "stewardship." "Stewardship is the keystone—the concept both organic and rational, flexible and systematic" ("Stegner" 96). Ronald believes that Stegner embraced stewardship "because our twentieth-century environmental and temporal circumstances have dictated such an alliance" (97). To complicate matters, it is important in this context to realize that among so many other roles that he took, Stegner was a historian. Leading figures from the history of environmentalism, such as Aldo Leopold and George Perkins Marsh, espoused stewardship, and they had a profound effect on his thinking, largely because he, unlike many declared environmentalists, was aware in detail of these pioneers' words and accomplishments and because he saw environmentalism not as the current political cause but as an ongoing struggle with a complex history.

Marsh, who wrote *Man and Nature,* warned in 1864 of the consequences of tampering with the environment, and he outlined how changes made by humans had affected plants, animals, and our physical surroundings. He pointed out the dangers, regretted the damage, and, in Ronald's words, suggested

> the importance of restored harmony between man and his natural
> surroundings. Like Powell, his ideas were dismissed in his own time
> but have been adopted and advocated by subsequent generations. His
> ideas are particularly relevant to Stegner, for they lead inherently to
> stewardship. Once man has altered the environment, he cannot stop
> doing so. (97)

In other words, as much as we may like to do so, there is no going back. We must pick up the pieces and go forward with, one hopes, a different definition of "progress." The sad thing is that Marsh was writing almost a century and a half ago, and Powell wrote his *Report on the Lands of the Arid Region of the United States* in 1878.

In her essay on Stegner, Ronald's approach is one of exposing the "real" position of Stegner, a position that she claims is fraught with contradictions. The contradictions in Stegner's environmentalist record are to a large extent the product of his growth and learning over time. Just as the environmental movement itself evolved and changed during those years of the 1950s, 1960s, and 1970s, so too did Stegner's position. As a child of the frontier, he found nature much more powerful than humans, so that the survival of humans, not nature, was the question. His sense of humans as a danger to nature had to develop over time as his situation and perspective changed—and as society and technology evolved. And as a child of the frontier, he came to admire those who with courage stuck through hard times and built communities. He came to admire those who could build with few resources, who could "make do" and "cobble things together," and thus his admiration for the engineer—a figure about whom he would develop mixed feelings later in life. He would come to admire the scientists, like John Wesley Powell, who tried to dispel the western myths of rugged individualism and the "Garden

West," but then later would develop some of the environmentalists' suspicion of the technological products of science.

Perhaps the one thing above all that Ronald sees as tarnishing Stegner's environmental record, raising doubts about his total commitment, and contradicting much that he has written is the book *Discovery!* As the history of the Arabian American Oil Company's (ARAMCO) discovery and development of the oil fields of Saudi Arabia, the book is indeed, as Ronald describes it, a story that focuses on engineers, engineering, and corporate and national exploitation of natural resources. Ronald is right—at face value; this was a strange book for an environmentalist to have written.

But the story behind the story makes the book understandable, if no less bothersome. To begin with, it should be said that it was commissioned by the oil company to be written as an "in-house" history to be distributed to employees and stockholders. When completed, the manuscript was withheld by the company because some of the executives did not feel it was very flattering. It was first published serially in abridged form (one might even say in censored form) in *ARAMCO World Magazine* (from January 1968 through July/August 1970). By that time Stegner was unhappy about the situation: the censorship irked him, and he felt double-crossed. The book, a collection of the articles, was published in 1971 and never put on sale to the general public.

This was not the first time Stegner accepted a commission. He had accepted one earlier from *Look* magazine to research and write *One Nation,* a collection of essays on prejudice in the United States. In both instances he was attracted to the assignment, but he was also partly motivated by the money. He was making little from his writing (and that mostly from his short stories rather than his books), and his salary at Stanford was low even as a full professor. The assignment to write the ARAMCO history was given to him on the basis of the company's connection to Stanford: most of its engineers were Stanford graduates, and several of the company's executives were admirers of Stegner's work. The company spared no expense in backing his research—everything was first-class. "It was," Stegner reflected, "kind of nice for an old English professor to operate in terms like that."

What attracted Stegner to the project itself was that it was the story of a group of men trying to build something on a frontier, a frontier as hostile and unforgiving as any on the planet. At the time, it was not in his mind a situation in which men were destroying nature so much as a situation in which they, working at the very edge of their ability to survive, were creating something valuable for an impoverished society. This was a history that seemed to be right up his alley, and researching it might be an adventure taking him to new places and introducing him to the sort of people he was unlikely to meet as an English teacher. Nevertheless, he was in doubt about it and asked his wife, Mary, whether they should go to Saudi Arabia or not. With dreams of *A Thousand and One Nights,* she exclaimed, "Oh, yes, let's do it."

But for Mary, it turned out not to be much of an adventure. She was not allowed to travel with her husband around the country during his research and was confined to a compound constructed for the company wives, where they had little to do but sit around a swimming pool listening to Musak and sipping soft drinks all day. Stegner did see much of the country, both by truck and by plane, and then when they returned to the States, he met a number of the pioneers, now retired.

The book makes clear that he did learn to admire these men, who displayed such courage and persistence. What he admired most, typically for him, was the cooperative effort that the engineers, mechanics, and construction workers had to make in order to overcome the obstacles of climate and terrain; the lack of proper materials, equipment, and trained workers, as well as the constrictions of Saudi Arabian laws, religious customs, and tribal traditions. These men seemed to him to demonstrate what pioneering cooperation could accomplish, as versus the individualism so often praised, if not always practiced, on the American frontier. But as Ronald points out, the book "glamorizes a process while dismissing its effects" ("Stegner" 94). Furthermore, as she also points out, here, as throughout much of Stegner's work, there is a thread of anthropocentrism, adopting a perspective of human needs and perceptions. For example, when speaking of Capitol Reef (which he recommended be made a national park when he was an assistant to the secretary of the interior), he says, "The land is not complete without its human history and associations. Scenery by itself is pretty sterile" (*American Places* 143).

It is Stegner the historian talking here, a man who saw topography in terms of human events. His son, Page, tells of many hours riding in the back seat of the car while his father made numerous trips throughout the West researching his histories. Page recalls that his father

could never just *look* at the scenery. If we happened to be driving across
the Colorado Plateau through southern Utah . . . he'd offer up an anec-
dote about Powell being rescued by Bradley in Desolation Canyon, and
then explain to his slightly annoyed eight-year-old boy (me), who was
trying to concentrate on his Batman comic, who Powell was and why he
was important. Then he'd point out the La Sals and Abajos to the south
and tell that boy something about laccolithic domes, betting him he
couldn't spell *laccolithic.* . . . Crossing over the Wasatch Plateau and
heading south through the Spanish Fork Canyon would remind him
of the specific dates of the Escalante/Dominguez expedition through
the region. ("A Brief" 29)

As this reminiscence suggests, Stegner would talk to his son and wife on such
trips not only about historical events but also at length about the geological
history of places as they encountered them. His intense interest in geology
was yet another reason why the ARAMCO project, which in part concerned
the activities and accomplishments of geologists, attracted him and another
reason why *science* was not for him a dirty word.

It may well be that *Discovery!* "glamorizes a process while dismissing its
effects," although it seemed to this reader that while reading the book, one
may become aware of certain implicit conflicts in its author. Stegner admires
progress but is suspicious of it, likes the can-do enthusiasm of the oil-field
workers but displays an underlying unease with a project so motivated by
exploitation of the land for money, even though the land is largely barren. In
other words he shows very human mixed emotions. As not only a teacher
but also a lifelong learner, he seldom displayed in his work the absolutist certainty of the environmentalist true believer. Although he was one of the
most influential advocates for wilderness preservation, he could engage in
advocacy only on the basis of human values.

In her evaluation of Stegner, Ronald is quite right to label his stance as
one of "stewardship," a stance that followed the lead of conservationist pioneers like Marsh and Leopold. The only problem is that although Ronald
does not say so, her tone implies that stewardship is not quite good enough.
It is true that viewed from the outside Wallace Stegner's environmental
record contains many apparent contradictions, but that record reflects the
man—it does not stand alone as the product of an agenda. While Stegner

was influenced in his thinking by many of his predecessors, as well as by contemporaries such as Bernard DeVoto, Ansel Adams, and Stewart Udall, his environmental ethic was shaped primarily by his personal experience. And in his reactions to that experience, he was consistent throughout his adult life. As Brett J. Olsen in his essay on Stegner's environmentalism states,

> He derived his primary understanding of the land from the empirical, practical fact of growing up in the West. His best environmental writings reflect this experience. As his early life fell at odds with romantic notions of the West, a skepticism regarding western myth lay at the core of his environmentalism. Indeed, perhaps more than any, Stegner understood, from both experience and observation, the environmental and human damage caused by blind adherence to frontier mythology. (125)

I would only add that it was not just growing up in the West that formed the basis of his environmentalism but also the natures of his father and mother, the boomer and the nester.

He became a realist, a thoroughgoing democrat, an inquirer into the history he had missed as a child on the frontier, and a supporter of the ideals of community and cooperation. These traits did not always lead him into the environmentalist purity that some would demand, but he followed his conscience wherever it led him. He lived a life that stretched from the time of the horse and plow and tar paper shacks built on an unforgiving prairie to the proliferation of suburbs and our evolution into the information age. As someone who worked hard as a steward to conserve and improve our environment, he had an almost unique perspective.

CHAPTER FIVE

Why I Can't Read Elizabeth Cook-Lynn

In 1996, three years after Wallace Stegner's death, a Sioux woman, Elizabeth Cook-Lynn, published a book titled *Why I Can't Read Wallace Stegner and Other Essays: A Tribal Voice.* Cook-Lynn is angry, very angry, with a host of grievances, and much of her anger is directed toward Wallace Stegner, as expressed in the title essay. It may be that in a general sense her hostility is justified—certainly the American Indian has been terribly victimized over the centuries: betrayed, exploited, condescended to, brutalized, and, sometimes even worse, ignored. But I would suggest that her rage is misdirected when she uses Wallace Stegner as her straw man and makes him into an icon of white ignorance and persecution. Furthermore, there is something cheap and underhanded in using Stegner's name and reputation in order to popularize and sell her book. She has slandered and falsely accused a good man.

Cook-Lynn seems to have settled on Stegner in the belief that as a white author who wrote largely about the West and who has been extremely popular, he would make a good target for her diatribe. By saying, "there are few of us [Americans] who have not read his works" (29), she begins with a misconception. As I did research on him for many years as his biographer, it became clear to me that although he may have gained popularity with a few, nine out of ten people across the country had never heard of him. He was no Stephen King, nor, certainly, was he a Louis L'Amour—who, by the way, might have been a better target as a perpetuator of the western myth that Stegner throughout his career fought to dispel. (At the same time, it should be said that while propagating the myth of the lone horseman, L'Amour, like many white writers of popular Westerns, made himself an expert on American Indian culture and history.) Stegner was revered not for his popularity or his western stories (he wrote only two short stories about cowboys) but for his honesty and compassion. Among other things, he cared about the Indians and had great sympathy for their plight.

Cook-Lynn admits that she has read only *Wolf Willow* and *Conversations with Wallace Stegner on Western History and Literature* (and she has not read these carefully). If she had done her homework on her target, she would have read a great deal more, including *One Nation*, Stegner's book of essays on prejudice and discrimination in our country. The collection was unusual for its time in that its topic was seldom pursued in mainstream publications in 1945. Stegner had been hired by *Look* magazine to write a series of articles on groups that had been the objects of discrimination, to be accompanied by photographs and eventually gathered into a book. Publication of the articles was so loaded with peril for the publisher (circulation in various parts of the country would certainly suffer) that it decided not to publish the essays in the magazine after all, choosing instead to publish them, somewhat softened, in book form. It was not a project that promised fame or advancement for the author.

In addition to essays about such groups as the Chinese, Japanese, Filipinos, Mexicans, Blacks, Jews, and Catholics, there was an essay titled "Least-Known Americans: Rebirth of the American Indian" in a section called "Oldest Americans." Stegner begins by pointing out that in the previous couple of decades (prior to 1943), the number of Indians had increased dramatically, "so much for the myth of the vanishing race." He continues,

> Reduced by the white man's bullets and bottles, and dying out until a generation ago, it is now increasing faster proportionately than any other group in the nation. . . . But while we were forgetting that Indians still existed, or trying to "Americanize" the remnants, they suffered almost as much from our indifference and our charity as they did earlier from our Manifest Destiny. (141)

Two items in this selection deserve notice in regard to Cook-Lynn's attack: Stegner's refutation of the "myth of the vanishing race" and his acknowledgment of Indian suffering at the hands of our doctrine of Manifest Destiny.

Cook-Lynn takes a phrase out of context from *Wolf Willow,* misreads it, and uses that misreading extensively in her attack on Stegner. The phrase (in a section on the history of the Indians in the border area between Canada and the United States) is "the Plains Indians were done." She states,

> Unfortunately, Stegner's theory is that as America rises, the Sioux Nation expires. We need only to look at Lithuania, at Poland, Bulgaria and other national groups involved in the reorganization of the former USSR in the 1990s to know that nations do not die simply because another nation has willed it so. (38)

Aside from the fact that the Sioux were never a nation in the European sense—the parallel is far-fetched—the idea that she attributes to Stegner is totally wrong. He did not, as the quotation above from *One Nation* demonstrates, see the Indians as expiring, nor would he have had any joy, contrary to what Cook-Lynn suggests, in such an expiration if it had happened.

When he says "the Plains Indians were done," he is not saying that the nation no longer existed; instead he is talking about the end, in July 1881, of the Sioux as a viable fighting force. Earlier, to escape the U.S. Cavalry and the cheating and abuse they had suffered in the States, several tribes crossed the "Medicine Line," or border, into Canada, where the indigenous tribes had received fairer treatment than had tribes in the United States (although Cook-Lynn does not believe it). But Canada, doubtful that the Indians would keep the peace, was not happy to see these new arrivals and refused to give them the treaty money that tribes native to Canada had received. Of these peoples, Sitting Bull and his followers were the most threatening; however, the authorities gradually whittled down Sitting Bull's power by never consulting him as head chief and instead going to others under him. In addition, the authorities persuaded more than twelve hundred of his followers to return to agencies south of the line. The buffalo were nearly gone, there was neither food nor money to buy food, and Sitting Bull's ranks were so depleted that a serious fight against the Canadian or American whites would have been impossible. In bitterness and quarreling over the few bags of flour left to them, the remaining Sioux

> made their scarecrow march southward through the whitened buffalo bones . . . [and] met Captain Clifford at the place now called Plenty-

wood, Montana. The day after that, the gates of Fort Bufford closed behind them and their guns were stacked in the yard and the Plains Indians were done. (*Wolf Willow* 120)

This, briefly, is the context of the phrase that Cook-Lynn takes such exception to, demonstrating that the phrase does not have the meaning she attributes to it.

In his recapitulation of the history of the Cypress Hills area of Saskatchewan, where he spent his childhood, there are three chapters entirely or partially devoted to the Indians: "The Medicine Line," "Law in a Red Coat," and "Capital of an Unremembered Past." Throughout these there is a detailed, matter-of-fact telling of events—a telling with a white perspective certainly, but an evenhanded one nevertheless.

Stegner's only departure from objectivity is not a gloating over the decline of Indian power but just the opposite—a pervasive sadness. This is his description of a group of Nez Percé who came to Canada, "refugees from Chief Joseph's long-running battle" in the States. They "limped in, wounded, exhausted, stripped of everything but horse and gun":

> They were White Bird and ninety-eight men, fifty women, and about fifty children, the battered remnant of a tribe that their conqueror General Miles called "the boldest men and best marksmen" he had ever known. They had been friends of the whites ever since Lewis and Clark first met them under their other name of Chopunnish. Half-Americanized, some of them Christians, house-dwellers, farmers, they had been cheated and abused until they made one of the last, the most desperate, and certainly one of the most heroic of the Indian revolts against the system that was destroying their life. (*Wolf Willow* 118)

That Cook-Lynn seems unaware of this sympathy suggests that she comes at Stegner with a knife and hardness in her heart and is unwilling to see anything but that which might be used against him. Is Stegner saying here that this group's "half-Americanization" was a good thing? No, he is emphasizing the severity of the betrayal.

Cook-Lynn does make a point against white continental history in general that Stegner would agree with: it has tended to romanticize white settlement and has tended not to give Native Americans their due. By contrast

Stegner may have sympathy for the Indians in his account, but his is a realistic depiction of events and situations. He does not glorify or sanctify white discovery or settlement. In his interview with Richard Etulain, Stegner discusses western history and historians, making the point that there has been too much romanticizing of the West: "I'm afraid that the romantic imagination has taken the West, and it's probably never going to let it go. You're always swimming upstream when you try to write something serious about the West" (Stegner and Etulain 152).

This comment brings up another Stegner remark, which he made on a number of occasions, that Cook-Lynn resents and dwells on: "Western history sort of stopped at 1890." Why she objects to this, how it might slander the American Indian, is not clear. She seems to think that he has declared the death of the Indian and a way of life: "Unless someone comes forward to say that Western history did not stop in 1890, Indians will forever be exempted from Descartes's admonition concerning humanity: 'I think, therefore I am'" (30). "In the imagination of the Sioux," she continues, "that moment of awful violence [the massacre at Wounded Knee] has meant the beginning of hard times, the basis for evidence of a long and glorious history, the focal point of survival" (30–31).

What we have here, again, is another example of what would seem to be purposeful misreading. A major theme throughout Stegner's essays and histories (as we have seen elsewhere in this volume) has been the refutation of western myths, one of which focuses only on one short period of western history. This is the period of a little more than a decade and a half of the Wild West, which has taken hold in our imaginations as *the* West, the period of free-ranging cattle and cattle barons, of shoot-outs and walk-downs. It is the "cowboy myth of rugged individualism, freedom, adventure, everybody's fantasy of being out alone with nature in wild colorful places. Most western lives are not like that" (Stegner and Etulain 163). In speaking of the "end of the West in 1890," Stegner is speaking about the end of the Wild West period of white settlement and emphasizing its brevity (compared to so much else western, including the continuity of American Indian culture) and the fact that in reality this period is not characteristic of the West as it was or is. Thus, he means just the opposite of what Cook-Lynn takes him to mean. His statement has nothing to do with the "death" of Indian "mythological continuity and primordial historiography" (Cook-Lynn 33).

What was Stegner's view of the Native Americans and their plight? To answer that question we should go back to *One Nation*. At the time of its writing in 1945, Stegner looked back over recent history to detect a dramatic change in white attitudes toward and treatment of the Indian. The "Americanization" programs of the reservation boarding schools and missionaries "aimed at eradicating the stubborn Indian heritage failed" because there was no place in the larger society for the white-educated Indian. For about a century, this forced Americanization "had gone well toward the end one writer describes: the reduction of all Indians to the status of 'outcasts, paupers, and psychopaths'" (142). Then in 1929 the Indian Service came up with a program (passed into law in 1934 as the Indian Reorganization Act) that promised to meet Indian needs. Behind this new program

> is a clear recognition of the Indian's right to personal dignity *as an Indian;* a belief that, given encouragement and a basis for pride and self-respect, Indians can go far toward rehabilitating themselves. . . . The new policy aims at restoring lands to tribal use, giving every tribe the opportunity of self-government, and encouraging all the arts, crafts, languages, and folkways which were discouraged under the earlier system. (142)

Not all Indians agreed with this policy, but it seems to me that Cook-Lynn might feel in reading Stegner's endorsement of the Indian's right to personal dignity "as an Indian" that he has been, at least in part, on her side.

Stegner was ahead of his time in rejecting the idea that every member of our society should be assimilated and in rejecting the idea that each of us should give up our cultural heritage. He was, although he does not use the word, endorsing our present concern that we preserve and encourage *diversity* in our society. By preserving diversity and bringing everyone together in pride in his or her own culture, we could, indeed, have one nation—we need not, should not, aim at homogenization. Forced Americanization of Indians has led only to demoralizing them because "at the bottom of all that teaching was the feeling that an Indian should be ashamed to be what he was. The new policy is removing that sense of shame, letting the Indian move in the world as an equal, though different citizen" (143). Of course, Stegner points to the ideal, the aim, which I am sure that Cook-Lynn would be the first to point out has not by any means been reached, even a half century later (and

Stegner himself notes that at the time of his writing prejudice against the first Americans still exists). But it is a noble aim, and Stegner should be given credit for endorsing it. He concludes his essay by saying, "We already owe the Indian so much that we might well consider learning more instead of trying to make a white man of him" (143).

Before and after his work on *One Nation,* Stegner was doing research for his history-biography, *Beyond the Hundredth Meridian: John Wesley Powell and the Second Opening of the West* (1954). He came to admire Powell very much during the course of his work, not only for his courage, his lifelong pursuit of knowledge, and his devotion to democracy, but also for his humanity. His was a giving and generous spirit, nearly without ego. Powell was an explorer and frontiersman of the best kind—the complete antithesis of what Stegner called the "boomer"; and Powell became interested in Native Americans and their cultures. He shared Stegner's concern that the Indians be able to retain their dignity and that their traditions be treated with respect. For decades Powell roamed throughout the West, exploring and surveying through Indian country, but he never carried a gun and never was threatened.

Back in Washington as head of the Geological Survey, he went on to establish the Bureau of Ethnology, where he was committed to discovering and preserving Native American cultures, languages, artifacts, and traditions. In other words he set out to discover and help to preserve the very cultural continuity that Cook-Lynn so values. It was important to him that no more of the Indian inheritance be lost, since through outright hostility, as well as ignorance and ethnocentricity, so much of it by that time already had been. Stegner notes in his biography of Powell that in regard to the Native Americans,

> Powell respected them and earned their respect, because he accepted
> without question their right to be what they were, to hold to the beliefs
> and institutions natural to them. To approach a strange culture and
> a strange people without prejudice, suspicion, condescension, or fear
> is common enough among students now; it was not too common
> in 1870. (131)

Stegner's discussion of Powell's establishment of the Bureau of Ethnology displays a considerable knowledge of Indian history. As usual, Stegner is the realist and impartial—he gives little credit to the whites in his account of the relationship of whites to the Native Americans. He begins by pointing out that in the mid–nineteenth century it seemed obvious to white Americans, "who by discovery, exploration, trade, bullets, rum, treaties, and the Word of God took over the continent from its aboriginal inhabitants," that those inhabitants were doomed to extinction, and soon. Of course, as Stegner points out, they were wrong. But strangely enough, the same people who participated in wronging the Indian could "quite honestly and even simulta-neously—denounce the juggernaut that was destroying him" (256). On the one hand, we were persuaded by the movement toward Manifest Destiny, which we believed was sanctioned by God, while on the other hand and at the same time, we were enshrining the figure of the noble savage and mourning his loss. Nevertheless, "however sympathetically or even senti-mentally a white American viewed the Indian, the industrial culture was cer-tain to eat away at the tribal cultures like lye" (256). What destroyed the Indian, Stegner points out,

> was not primarily political greed, land hunger, or military power, not the white man's germs or the white man's rum. What destroyed him was the manufactured products of a culture, iron and steel, guns, needles, woolen cloth, things that once possessed could not be done without. And the de-struction visited upon the Indian was not precisely or always what the public thought it would be. It was not the literal extermination of the race. [Cook-Lynn take note.] . . . It was not the continuity of the Indian race that failed; what failed was the continuity of the diverse tribal cul-tures. (256)

And this failure in the continuity in tribal cultures was the problem that Powell faced as he attempted to research those cultures in order to identify and systematically categorize them.

There were peoples, such as the Pueblo and Navajo in the surviving Indian country of the Southwest, who could give living testimony. But in the eastern part of the continent, the cultures of these Indians "were either extinct or so altered, debased, interpenetrated and diluted and mixed one with another and with white civilization that much of the ethnologist's work was all but archaeological" (257). Furthermore, four centuries of warfare and cultural exchange had moved many tribes from their ancestral homes and even moved them clear out of one culture into another. The discovery, then, of what had been before these changes and what remained "was a subject to excite a scholarly mind, especially a mind galvanized by evolutionary science and tempted by the nineteenth-century exercise of synthesizing and codifying human knowledge" (258).

Powell wanted to systematize the study of the American Indian, a study long neglected. And like Stegner, he was a realist, a myth buster. Up to the time that Powell began his work, with the backing of the Smithsonian, the study of the Indians had been

> cluttered with the guesses of amateurs and the mythology of wishful thinking of Welshmen, Mormons, and popular romancers, conducted out of ignorance into fabrication, clouded with blood and old feuds, burdened with the missionary zeal that wanted to put all Indians into overalls with hoes in their hands, complicated by governmental bad faith and misunderstanding and by Indian hatred and instability. (258)

This breaking through myth and fabrication to the truth of the actual structures and institutions of Indian ethnic groups was one of the two great works of Powell's life. And even after he was forced out as head of the Geological Survey, he continued with his ethnological studies. By the end of his life, "he and his bureau had remade the science of cultural anthropology as thoroughly as the Powell Survey earlier had remade—or made—the science of physiography" (259).

Cook-Lynn really hates *Wolf Willow,* published in 1962, eight years after *Beyond the Hundredth Meridian.* Everything about it irritates her, and there is hardly any detail in it concerning Stegner's motives in writing the book that does not set her off on a tirade. Always interested in cooperation and community, Stegner had a decade earlier gotten the idea for a book comparing small communities in terms of their histories and how they were organized and how they functioned. He planned to compare the culture of a European village that had been in existence for many centuries with that of both an American village that had been in existence for more than two centuries and a village that had come into being just recently on the frontier. He thought he might use Hardanger, Norway, where his mother's family had come from, or perhaps an even older village he had located in Denmark; Greensboro in Vermont, where he had a summer home; and Eastend in

Saskatchewan, where he had spent his childhood. The book would be essentially an effort to locate himself, a historical exploration by a man who felt that while growing up he had been deprived of history.

He felt that as a child in Eastend he had been educated for the wrong place—"education tried, inadequately and hopelessly, to make a European of me" (*Wolf Willow* 24). Living in the Cypress Hills (the area surrounding Eastend in Saskatchewan), he did not even know that he lived there:

> [I] hadn't the faintest notion of who had lived there before me. But I could have drawn you a crudely approximate map of the Baltic, recited you Tom Moore songs or Joaquin Miller's poem on Columbus, or given you a rudimentary notion of the virtues of the Gracchi or the misfortunes of the Sabine women. (27)

In order to start on his comparison-of-villages project and to recover a sense of his own personal background, Stegner with his wife went back in 1953 on an extended trip to Eastend, a place he had not seen since 1920. He talked to local old-timers, spent time with back issues of the town newspaper, and walked down the paths he had followed to school and to the swimming hole thirty years earlier.

Still pursuing his idea of a comparison of villages, he went to Europe the following year but found that the language barrier made it impossible for him to probe with any depth into the history of a European village in Denmark or Norway. He changed the project to one in which he would concentrate on telling of the discovery of his own history and the history of the place where his childhood took place. The book's form gradually came together as an eclectic mixture of materials, as indicated by its subtitle, *A History, a Story, and a Memory of the Last Plains Frontier.*

Stegner's goal of finding out who had lived in the Cypress Hills before him would seem to be a understandable and modest one. However, Cook-Lynn is outraged that Stegner should dare to assume a history that was not his—as a European descendent he should focus only on the history of his family in Norway. According to her, when he mourns the fact that his schooling "tried, inadequately and hopelessly, to make a European out of [him]," he is "ironically and sadly disposing of the only legitimate legacy he and other immigrant children could claim" (31). She points to his comment about the Cypress Hills area—"if I am native to anything I am native to this"—and states that this "personalization takes place in the imagination, thus the claim to identity needs only acclamation," and that "the substance of what Stegner imagines becomes believable to everyone except those who have had thousands of years of prior knowledge of that same world and environment and imagined on their own very different terms." She wonders if Stegner ever "grasped the final immorality of [his] . . . position" (30).

Cook-Lynn's self-righteous diatribe against Stegner raises a number of questions. To whom does history belong? Only to those whose ancestors have lived in an area for "thousands of years" (as Cook-Lynn constantly reminds us about her ancestors)? But we are all immigrants (as she likes to call all white people in America). God did not put the Indians down in the middle of North America and tell them This is your land; no one else can live here. If Cook-Lynn wants Stegner to go back to Norway, one might ask her to go back to Siberia-Mongolia. Peoples have moved from place to place and across the globe since the beginning of humankind. Sometimes they occupied open spaces, sometimes they displaced other peoples, and sometimes they absorbed others. What happened to the American Indians, as regrettable and tragic as it may have been, was not unique in human history. And what happened is not, as Cook-Lynn suggests, equivalent to either Apartheid in South Africa or the Holocaust in Europe.

Stegner states that his people believed "this country was a new country, and a new country had no history." He adds that "the world when I began to know it had neither location nor time, geography, nor history." He says these things in order to show how ignorant he was and that he and other settlers were completely wrong, but Cook-Lynn takes these statements at face value and says, "Claiming ignorance, Stegner can say that the final curtain has fallen [which, as I point out above, he does not say], no handprints of any human perpetrator can be found, criminal action requires no reprimand" (31). If we are talking about the Cypress Hills, the area was not without history, but the evidence so far shows that it was nearly without inhabitants most of the time throughout history. The Sioux, or Dakotas, Cook-Lynn's tribe, did not claim this territory and were only there briefly, when Sitting Bull brought his followers out of the United States into Canada to escape the cavalry. But Stegner grew up there. Who has more claim to an interest in the area's history? Cook-Lynn claims that Stegner denies her history, but it would seem to be the other way around.

Whether they have had ancestors in a place for thousands of years or only a few, people have always resented the outsider, the newcomer. I am a third-generation Californian (going back more than a hundred years to immigrants from Germany), and it has been hard for me not to resent newcomers who have brought their values and traditions (along with horrendous traffic jams) into my community. A neighbor moved in from Georgia and proceeded to fly the Confederate battle flag over his front yard. I was tempted to tell him to go home or take that flag down—California was part of the Union—but I did not. In this country he had as much right to be here as I did and a perfect right through his freedom of speech to express his values (as much as I deplored those values of declared racial superiority). It may be that Cook-Lynn also has the right to express her values, but one has to ask about those values whether her unqualified hatred of white Americans is a variety of racism.

It is amusing but also sad to see people who have barely been in California a decade deeply resenting those newcomers just coming in to settle. Back in the Depression, a half million immigrants came from the Dust Bowl into California bringing their values and traditions, their dress and speech, with them. Most came from subsistence farms, and life in California, with its urban culture and industrialized agriculture, was completely foreign to them. Native Californians were astonished to confront thousands of impoverished people who had never seen a flush toilet, and Californians began to talk of them, and treat them, as animals. At first welcomed to provide surplus farm labor and thus low wages, they were finally deeply resented, even hated; and most Californians wanted them to go home or somehow to disappear into the sea. It was common for counties, after the picking was over, to provide gasoline to the migrants if they would promise to go back home. Should we tell the children or grandchildren of the Okies that they must not study the history of California—it is not theirs? Does that history belong only to the indigenous Indians?

How about the resentment toward the Mexican immigrants who seem to be on their way toward overwhelming the present white majority? And how about the counter-resentment by the Mexicans who claim California as theirs going back to 1822? Claims and counterclaims, hatreds and counterhatreds. Will we allow ourselves to be caught up in a constant cycle of racial and ethnic conflict, arguing, as in the Balkans, for centuries over who owns what history; or have we developed a different kind of country where we can live together, in justice, without grudges or festering wounds?

Just as most Americans would admit that slavery was wrong (and most had ancestors that either had nothing to do with it or actively opposed it), most would admit that the American Indians, on the whole, had been wronged (although most—including tens of millions of nonwhite immigrants and tens of millions of recent white immigrants—had nothing to do with it). The picture is far more complex than the victims-villains picture that Cook-Lynn draws for us. She perpetuates her own myth of the West. She accuses Stegner of "serving the interests of a nation's fantasy about itself" (29). But hers is the fantasy, not Stegner's, a fantasy of perpetual victimization and guilt, of a continuing nineteenth-century conflict of Indians versus settlers (no wonder she objects to Stegner's stating that the Wild West ended in 1890), that can only inflame relations. How can we heal the wounds? I do not think we can do so by wounding others (or their reputations after they are dead) or by denying them their heritage or the legitimacy of their lives and works. Our country and its history belong to all of us, even if we just got off the boat; and we can be proud that among us are those whose history on this continent goes back thousands of years and who have given all of us so much. As Wallace Stegner might well have asked—what can we give back?

···

CHAPTER SIX

Finding a Voice of His Own
The Story of Wallace Stegner's Fiction

Writers are far more cunning than the credulous reader supposes. We are all practiced shape-shifters and ventriloquists; we can assume forms and speak in voices not our own. We all have to have in some degree what Keats called negative capability, the capacity to make ourselves at home in other skins.

WALLACE STEGNER
"The Law of Nature and the Dream of Man: Ruminations on the Art of Fiction," 1992

There are many ways to describe a career as long and diverse as that of Wallace Stegner, but one way, certainly, is to see it as the search for an effective narrative voice. What Stegner had to learn, and it took him three decades to learn it, was how to tell a story in his own way, to project a persona that spoke to the reader in a style and tone that was unmistakably his own. As a private man, he was at first reluctant to risk revealing himself in his fiction and spoke to his readers in an anonymous voice that maintained a considerable distance from both audience and material. What followed was a slow evolution through an uneven career in writing fiction toward the creation of a fictive personality with a voice that can be seen to be at the heart of his success in the last, great period of his work, when he won both the National Book Award and the Pulitzer. It was a voice very personal, yet fictional—as Wallace Stevens might say, "He sang a song of himself, yet not himself."

Of course when we use the term "voice," we are speaking figuratively, just as when we use "speak" or "talk" in writing, we are using a metaphor that assumes a vocalization on some level by both the writer and the reader. In his book *Fiction's Inexhaustible Voice: Speech and Writing in Faulkner* (1989), Stephen M. Ross provides this basic definition of how we ordinarily use the term:

> The word "voice" has been employed traditionally as a metonymic designation for the human presence we hear or imagine whenever we read a poem or a story. In its commonsensical way "voice" signifies expressive "sound" in literary speech, those inscribed, perceivable differences among characters' talking, among narrators' story telling, and among authors' styles. (4)

I am going to refer to voice in terms of style, as well as point of view and authorial distance. But mainly, however, as a biographer I am interested in voice as the artistically fashioned expression of a person, the author, which in this case evolved over time to be a more complete expression of the author as it became more personal. At the same time as voice in Stegner's fiction moved closer to become a more accurate expression of the author, it became more effective as a literary expression—most notably in its increased credibility, in its forcefulness of presentation, and in its power to intellectually challenge readers and entertain them.

John Fowles has said, "The long evolution of fiction has been very much bound up with finding means to express the writer's 'voice'—his humors, his private opinions, his nature—by means of word manipulation and print alone" (Ross 6). As we know from such studies as Ian Watt's classic *The Rise of the Novel* (1957) and Lennard J. Davis's *Factual Fictions: The Origins of the English Novel* (1983), the earliest novelists—Samuel Richardson and Daniel Defoe—sensed the importance of making their fictions credible and did so by pretending that these fictions were real documents—journals, diaries, or letters. By assuming the guise of a particular voice, these novelists wanted to persuade their audiences that a real person had recorded real events. But with the appearance on the scene of Henry Fielding, the reportorial voice is replaced by the authorial voice, a voice that convinces by its tone and colloquial syntax that a real storyteller exists behind the story. So convincing is it, that in *Joseph Andrews* and *Shamela*, Fielding uses the latter voice to make fun of the former and its reportorial pretensions. We are taken up by a *personality*—by an author pretending successfully to be someone (by sounding like someone) rather than by a fiction pretending to be a document. Throughout its history, fiction has tended to gain acceptance from its readers on the basis of whether it involves and affects them—that is, if the distance between novel and reader has been reduced by the manner of its telling—and if we look back, we can see that the most enduring fictional works have usually been those that speak to us, whether they be by Fielding, Jane Austen, Charles Dickens, or William Faulkner. What Stegner had to learn, in short, was how to draw close the connection between story and audience as Fielding and others had been able to do.

Almost all of this, although a matter of common sense, is disputed or cast aside as irrelevant by much modern theory, which wants to ignore both author and reader in favor of language analysis in an effort to make the study of literature somehow akin to science. "There is nothing outside the text," according to Jacques Derrida, and to discuss "voice" is to indulge in the "phono-logical" fallacy (Jefferson 107). One of the few philosopher-critics who have recognized both the artistic and human dimensions of literature is Mikhail Bakhtin. In Bakhtin, the author lives: "The writer is a person who knows how to work language while remaining outside of it; he has the gift of indirect speech" (quoted in Lodge 7). This comment is reminiscent of Stegner's frequent reference to himself in his later years as a ventriloquist. Just as Bakhtin refers to the novel as a dialogue with many voices produced by an author outside the work, so too may the ventriloquist have many dummies, take on many roles that may authentically represent the various sides of his or her personality. None of these voices need be, according to Bakhtin, subject to the authoritarian control of the writer. The writer may create "not voiceless slaves . . . but rather free people who are capable of standing beside their creator, of disagreeing with him, and even rebelling against him"—which is precisely a description of the ventriloquist's act (Bakhtin 4). It is the independence of the dummies that makes the act an artistic creation and that provides that sense of authenticity, which makes it amusing to the audience.

But I would move beyond Bakhtin and extend the Stegner metaphor further: neither the personality (voice) of the ventriloquist in this dialogue nor the personality of the dummy is that of the ventriloquist as a person in life. Each voice is projection, an amplified, created version of the host personality. It is here that I part from Bakhtin: I would place an emphasis on voices as a fictional version of the self, a projection created out of the author's personality. As a biographer, I am interested in the artistic process, how and why that voice (or those voices) is created and how it may change over time; Bakhtin is interested in the artistic product, the dialogue itself, as a reflection of society and a reflection with political implications: language is seen "as the material medium in which people interact in society" (Forgacs 160). But there is one other area of my agreement with Bakhtin that should be mentioned before we move on: he distinguishes between the author's authoritarian voice, as in Tolstoy's novels, which he calls "monologic," and the dialogic conflict of voices, as in Dostoevsky's novels, which he calls "polyphonic" and which he considers superior. Roughly speaking, Stegner's greater success with the novel came as he moved from the authoritarian voice (with its penalty of distance) in the monologic early novels to the polyphony (with its bonuses of intimacy and conviction) of the later (Forgacs 163; Lodge 21).

Perhaps the best exposition of voice as I will use the term here is presented in the work of Albert J. Guerard, in his *The Triumph of the Novel: Dickens, Dostoevsky, Faulkner* (1976). He writes,

> The concept is of a "personal voice" discoverable in the work of every truly original writer: a voice that is the intimate and often unconscious expression of his temperament and unborrowed personality, a voice that in its structures and rhythms reflects the way his mind moves, and reflects too the particular needs and resistances of his spirit. (136)

Stegner's early novels—*Remembering Laughter* (1937), *On a Darkling Plain* (1940), and *Fire and Ice* (1941)—could have been written by nearly anyone— that is, they are well-written, but there is little that is distinctive about them. It is only with the later work—*All the Little Live Things* (1967), *Angle of Repose* (1971), *The Spectator Bird* (1976), and *Crossing to Safety* (1987)—that the author achieves, through the creation of voices to which he is able to commit himself closely and personally, his true originality.

I

The road toward the creation of an individualized, convincing, and forceful voice was for Stegner a long and hard one, with wrong turns, detours, and potholes. To summarize, his career began with a success, a prize-winning novelette, then faltered with two undistinguished works, and then was revived with *The Big Rock Candy Mountain* (1943), in which he changed directions toward the semi-autobiographical. After telling his own story, he tried in midcareer to figure out in which direction he should turn, wavering, as he tried one approach and then another. His career came to a point of crisis. He felt he was getting nowhere. He was so discouraged in his effort to transcend the autobiographical (my analysis of the problem, not his) that he gave up writing novels for ten years. In 1950, he had written *The Preacher and the Slave* (later titled *Joe Hill*), and as he recalls

> I gave up writing novels after *Joe Hill*. That book got a feeble press and no notice and didn't sell anything, and nobody understood it. . . . I thought, "Oh, Christ, I'm throwing pearls before swine and sounding off in the wilderness where there are no receivers tuned in. This is hopeless?" and so I just quit writing fiction. (Stegner and Etulain 72–73)

During that decade of the fifties, he did continue to write some short stories, however, and it was largely through their agency that he worked his way toward that narrative approach and distinctive voice that brought him to his greatest achievements. Some writers, like Hemingway and Faulkner, find and develop their voices early; others, like Stegner, find theirs late, so that their best work comes closer to the end rather than to the beginning of their careers.

Wallace Stegner began to write, as many another writer has, without any consciously developed plan of attack and with little knowledge of technique. It would seem to have been sheer talent that produced the prize-winning short novel *Remembering Laughter*, a story that had come to him through his wife's family about Iowa neighbors. The novelette's success—it won the Little, Brown novelette prize of $2,500—catapulted him suddenly onto the national scene in 1937 while he was an assistant professor at the University of Wisconsin. The prize had a downside as well as an up, since he had not really learned his craft and had been launched into fame before he was ready. Yet, he was driven forward by both a need to write, which had manifested itself as early as his undergraduate years at the University of Utah, and a Depression-era salary that was depressingly low.

Two forgettable novels followed, *On a Darkling Plain* (1940) and *Fire and Ice* (1941). Stegner was learning his trade but was compelled by necessity to push harder to follow up his original success than he should have. Neither of these novels, although in some of their details they depend on personal experience, can be thought of as autobiographical. They, along with *Remembering Laughter,* suggest a writer who, out of modesty and a sense of privacy, has distanced himself from his work, writing without deep feeling or personal involvement. We see this in his use of point of view. *On a Darkling Plain* and *Fire and Ice* depend on a third-person, limited omniscient point of view, and the voice of the narrator is singularly dispassionate and remote. We are not led to participate so much as to stand back and observe—to appraise rather than to feel the emotional condition of the central characters. These early novels seem to be the product of a writer who, instead of observing life, is looking to other novels for inspiration. In short, when we read, we are liable to think of his characters as book people, as romantic, as playing roles.

On a Darkling Plain, as we saw in chapter 2, is about a young Canadian veteran of World War I who has been invalided out of the army. Edwin Vickers returns bitter and disillusioned. Although he has a wealthy mother and family home in Vancouver, he decides to escape from society, taking up a homestead on the sparsely populated prairies of Saskatchewan. On his way to his isolated post on the plains, he stops at a small town to buy provisions. Barely polite to those he meets, he feels an intolerance even toward the people who mean well and are kindly toward him. His hard shell is cracked a bit when after a few months spent mostly alone he falls in love with the daughter of his nearest neighbor. The climax comes when she becomes ill and then dies during the 1918 flu epidemic, and her death drives Vickers back into angry isolation. However, after he too is stricken, he is led by her memory to devote himself to helping the community in its crisis.

At first, what stands out in the telling of this story is the contrast between the power of Stegner's presentation of those things that he knows about and the weakness of those things that he does not—a contrast he surely must have felt himself. Having grown up on a homestead farm in Saskatchewan, he knows what the plains look like, the touch and feel of their heat and dryness, and what it means to be lonely. What he does not convince us of is that he has an accurate sense of what thoughts may be generated in a mind consumed with self-hate and bitterness, nor does he convince us that Vickers's war experiences, as horrible as they may have been (and he gives us no details about this), could have caused such complete misanthropy.

Almost the same judgments can be made about *Fire and Ice.* The setting is the campus of the University of Wisconsin, which the author knows well; but the action concerns a student radical, Paul Condon, who, like Vickers, is angry with nearly everyone around him. Once again Stegner does not present a mind in which we can believe completely. Furthermore, Condon's sudden transformation into a more loving person at the end of the novel seems to show the same lack of conviction that Vickers's sudden conversion to concern for community shows. As in *On a Darkling Plain,* we seem to have a book written to illustrate an idea—the need for humans to move from rugged individualism to caring and community—and that idea is carried out rather stiffly, impersonally. In *Fire and Ice* the failure is not solely one of lack of experience. Stegner had gone to meetings of the Young Communist League and had closely observed people like Paul Condon, young people who were going to improve the world not because they really cared about others but because they had a chip on their shoulders. But the author, for all his observation, does not establish a sympathetic connection with their state of mind.

This distancing, this lack of connection suggests that with both Vickers and Condon, Stegner's failure was one of lack of commitment, an unwillingness to risk plumbing the self in order to release the creative imagination. In the greatest of stories and plays, the author seems to wholly take the part of each significant character—sympathetic or unsympathetic, regardless of age, sex, and race. Characters do not remain "other" but are embraced totally in their heroism, villainy, or ordinariness. Experience and the sensitivity to experience are important, but it all comes down to how an author uses experience and how much of his own feelings and psyche he is willing to risk. Stegner was an extremely intelligent man, as testified to by his brilliance in school, by the quality and variety of his publications, and by the testimony of colleagues and students, but he had to learn during this early period of his career that writing a successful novel is more than an intellectual exercise.

There is a tendency for scholars—and readers in general—to associate the people and events in a novel with the novelist's life. The novelist, in turn, usually denies that association, claiming instead that the work is the product of his or her imagination. But in such denials of correlation between the novelist's life and art there is often an element of disingenuousness—the workings of the artist's imagination must have a strong basis in life. Indeed, the stronger the basis, in the broadest sense, very often the more credible the result, not in the superficial sense of "belief" in character or event but in a deeper sense of recognition. Whether a novel is set in history or in some fantastic future, we feel we know the "truth" when we see it. We do not have these recognitions often in the early Stegner novels, and what is required is what might be called "a deeper presence."

In an illustration of the point, Henry James was often criticized as "bloodless" or, as H. G. Wells put it, "the culmination of the Superficial type" (248), but in his best work, he is just the opposite. Like Stegner, James uses the third-person, limited omniscient point of view, and in a work like *The Ambassadors*, he commits himself totally to the heart and soul of the central character, Strether. All those things that we usually use to delineate a character are only lightly touched on—we have only a dim consciousness of Strether's past, his appearance, his physical mannerisms. But in the long run these things matter little. By tracing Strether's thoughts—his values, his confusions, his mixed emotions, his false conclusions, his believable integrity, his naïveté—we learn to "know" him very well indeed. The author's "deep presence" in this character gives him lifelike dimensions and force, and that, in turn, makes *The Ambassadors* a great novel. James *is* Strether, although Strether is not James.

We "know" the character because we are led to feel that the author "knows": to paraphrase Robert Frost, he is not merely "acquainted." The easiest and surest way to achieve a deeper presence is to turn to autobiography, a path whose advantages Stegner certainly sensed, even if he did not make it a conscious choice. The direction taken by James, a more difficult one that went beyond autobiography, was in Stegner's career a choice delayed. Gradually Stegner's work focused more and more on his own feelings and experiences in growing up, more and more on his own family and circumstances, those things and people that moved him, still filled him with joy or pain.

II

Stegner's first significant entry into the autobiographical came with a story, "Bugle Song," composed in early 1937, before *Remembering Laughter* was published and won its prize in September of that year.[1] As we saw in chapter 3, the story deals with a farm boy on the prairie who leads a dual life, representing a conflict in roles that he does not yet recognize. Alone, except for his mother (the father is presumably out on the farm working), he divides his time between trapping gophers and killing them, feeding them to his pet weasel, on the one hand, and reading lyric poetry and dreaming of distant places, on the other. Hard and insensitive to the suffering of animals, he seems to perform his grisly task of ridding the farm of pests as part of the process of growing up into the masculine frontier role. His mother protests his cruelty, but he ignores her.

Similar contrasts between male and female roles, between insensitive and sensitive, caring and uncaring, are carried on as the themes in a series of stories about this boy that followed, stretching through the period in which *On a Darkling Plain* and *Fire and Ice* were published and up to 1943, when the novel, *The Big Rock Candy Mountain,* that contained most of these stories came out. The success of the initial stories in the series led to the idea for the novel. Reading these stories one after another, we can see how Stegner moves closer and closer to the bone, to his own sense of life as it was formulated on the Saskatchewan frontier, to what became important to him.

In an essay titled "Technique as Discovery," Mark Schorer argues that "the writer capable of the most exacting technical scrutiny of his subject matter, will produce works with the most satisfying content, works with thickness and resonance, works which reverberate" (168). Stegner's progress at this point in his career is an example of how the process might proceed in precisely the opposite direction—how the content that reverberates in the mind of the writer may well bring a more "exacting technical scrutiny" and how advances in technique may follow from a deeper participation. Comparing passages is bound to involve some unfairness, but allowing for that, it will still be helpful for illustrating my point to compare in a general way the distances between author and material in two segments and to see the resulting ease and conviction, the technical superiority, that come out of a closer engagement in the semi-autobiographical passage. Let us first look at a passage of meditation-description from *On a Darkling Plain:*

> Vickers mused on the doctor's words. The curiosity of people was a
> strange thing. He could stand it in individuals. O'Malley's [the doctor's]
> questions had not made him bristle. . . . But this matter of curiosity in

pack, this ganging together to strip everyone not strictly what the pack thought he ought to be, angered him like a pebble in a shoe. So damned empty themselves that they had to empty everyone else and paw among the entrails. (67)

The writer seems to be in unfamiliar territory, groping for effective language but ending up with a cliché ("pebble in a shoe") and a graceless metaphor ("paw among the entrails"). The failure of metaphor is a failure of imagination, and the failure of imagination here, it could be argued, stems from a lack of participation.

By contrast, here again is the beginning paragraph of "Bugle Song," wherein the narrator is presenting the sensations and thoughts of the boy:

There had been a wind during the night, and all the loneliness of the world had swept up out of the southwest. The boy had heard it wailing through the screens of the sleeping porch where he lay, and he had heard the washtub bang loose from the outside wall and roll down toward the coulee, and the slam of the screen doors, and his mother's padding feet after she rose to fasten things down. Through one half-open eye he had peered up from his pillow to see the moon skimming windily in a luminous sky; in his mind he had seen the prairie outside with its woolly grass and cactus white under the moon, and the wind, whining across that endless oceanic land, sang in the screens, and sang him back to sleep. (13)

Both Vickers and the boy are fictional characters, the boy no less than the man. But here, as this passage indicates, the author was able to take the part of the boy: his participation is complete, as one can see in the fresh images, the carefully chosen language, and the beautifully balanced phrasing. He feels what the boy is shown to feel—and expresses it through a voice that finds its truth by that feeling. Unlike the previous one, this second passage draws, almost forces, the reader to join the boy in his condition and the emotions accompanying that condition. The superiority of the second passage is not the result of improvement in technique over time—Stegner learning his craft—since it was written *before* the passage from *On a Darkling Plain.* An author's deeper participation can bring forth superior technique, and that is the great advantage of semi-autobiographical fiction. The superiority is not necessary, but more often, for most writers, possible.

This story and six others formed the foundation for the publication in 1943 of Stegner's semi-autobiographical novel *The Big Rock Candy Mountain,* the most successful book of the first half of his career. It takes the figure—who Stegner variously calls "the boy," "David," and "Bruce" in the stories, settling on Bruce Mason in the novel—and traces his life from early childhood until young manhood and the death, first, of his mother and then of his father. It is a long book, more than six hundred pages, and an immensely rich one, overflowing with anecdotes and autobiographical detail. Just how rich a vein Stegner had tapped is suggested by the fact that he had to cut more than two hundred pages from the beginning of the novel. In spite of this wealth of material, once he was through with the novel, he went back to his roots only rarely—a couple of short stories and the history-memoir-fiction combination called *Wolf Willow* (1962).

He took a long time (more than four years) to write the autobiographical novel that most modern writers seem bound to write and which is usually their first book; for some, it is their only major work. It would seem that these latter writers have been trapped, caught in their own lives and wondering where to go. Once writers get through their memories of growing up, where do they go for material? Some, like Zora Neale Hurston stay with their lives and ongoing experience; others, like Norman Mailer, immerse themselves in the currents of their culture; still others, like William Styron, go back into history. After a long struggle with this first major work, Stegner turned first in one direction and then in another—to ongoing experience, history, and cultural criticism. But then, realizing at last, after years of only mediocre success, that material alone was not the answer, he gradually, and tentatively at first, began to search for his voice. A somewhat different matter.

III

The Big Rock Candy Mountain sold well and got excellent notices. Once again, as when he won his prize for his first book, he thought his career was ready to take off. His next book, *Second Growth,* came out of a story he heard and people he had come to know in the town near his summer home in Vermont. But the novel achieved only moderate success, and he turned next to history, writing a fictionalized biography of labor martyr Joe Hill. *The Preacher and the Slave,* as the book was first called, was the product of an intense period of research and an enormous amount of hard work. The novel, however, is a cold one. The author keeps his distance from the material throughout, and although there is much in the book that might be of interest to a western history buff, there is little to warm the cockles of the heart.

Another way of stating the problem that Stegner faced at midcareer is Where do you go for funds once the memory bank has been exhausted? This question would seem an almost typically American one, since so many of our writers of fiction turn to autobiographical material early in their careers and find success with it. The ability to grow and transcend the autobiographical at some point, to go on to other material and to adopt another voice, can be seen as a critical turning point in the work of a number of our writers. Some, like Thomas Wolfe and J. D. Salinger, would seem to have been incapable of making the change; others, like Ernest Hemingway and Saul Bellow made it successfully. Still others, like Mark Twain and Sherwood Anderson, made the change, but not with total success: they are both remembered primarily for their books about growing up.

Stegner was able to find his way only gradually. The book that broke the dry spell, *A Shooting Star,* was not the answer. He struggled with it, had more correspondence with his publishers about it than about any other novel he wrote—a measure of his continuing sense of uncertain direction. The novel was inspired by a wealthy family of his acquaintance; their attitude and behavior had prompted him to an examination of our culture and its values. Despite his skillful handling of materials, some marvelous writing—he was really working very hard with this one—and several thought-provoking themes, the novel, about a wealthy woman having an identity crisis, seems to be an all-too-conscious attempt to break through previous barriers to achieve a best seller. There is nothing wrong with that, perhaps, but the book does seem to be, in retrospect, alien in matter and manner to Stegner's other fiction. It feels artificial; it seems to lack that "Stegner quality" of total conviction that marks his best work. It was a "come-back" book, one that did not take him in the right direction.

In the meantime, Stegner was laying a foundation in stories for the great period of his late work—*All the Little Live Things, Angle of Repose,* and *The Spectator Bird*—just as he had preceded his triumph with *The Big Rock Candy Mountain* by a foundation laid in a series of short stories about his childhood in Saskatchewan. In these later novels, as well as in his final one, *Crossing to Safety,* Stegner uses a first-person narrator to achieve a voice close to his own yet fictional, a voice that would convey a sense of truth and conviction that came not, as in *Big Rock,* out of the telling of his own story but rather out of the force of his personality and belief—and, one might add, his willingness to give up authoritarian control and let his characters breathe.

When asked in an interview if the voice of Joe Allston (who is the first-person narrator of two of these novels) was close to his own, Stegner replied, "Yes, but . . . don't read him intact. He goes further that I would. Anybody is likely to make characters to some extent in his own image" (Stegner and Etulain 77). One of many friends who have found the narrator close to the author, Mrs. R. E. Cameron (who knew him for forty-five years) said "Oh, yes" when asked "Do you think that part of him is this irascible storyteller you see in his late novels?"[2] He may take on another guise, go further, speak more frankly than he would in life, but the voice is his. Stegner was a man of old-fashioned virtues—polite, courteous, kind—who usually repressed the kind of witty sarcasm that his first-person narrators are likely to voice. In that sense, Joe Allston might be called an "extreme Stegner," saying and doing the things that Stegner in life might have been prompted to say and do, but did not.

The first tentative step, certainly taken unconsciously, toward the achievement of this voice came in a short story titled "The Women on the Wall" published just after World War II.[3] The story features a Mr. Palmer, a retired man of late middle age, who is writing his memoirs in a house near the Pacific Ocean. He is courtly in manner and, even in 1945, seems out of his time in a present more violent, more full of conflict, less genteel, less polite than he seems to expect. Instead of writing, he spends much of his time looking out the window—a habit that reminds us of Joe Allston, his successor in a later story, "A Field Guide to the Western Birds."

Revealed not in the first person, but in the third-person, limited omniscient point of view that had been a Stegner favorite, the center of consciousness, Mr. Palmer, is nevertheless the earliest appearance of what might be called the elderly writer-observer figure. He is an observer of people, experienced, sensitive to his environment, a bit skeptical and self-doubting, and despite a somewhat hardened shell, vulnerable to emotion—all qualities that would be carried over, although in somewhat different proportions, to Joe Allston in "Field Guide," *All the Little Live Things,* and *The Spectator Bird;* to Lyman Ward in *Angle of Repose;* and to Larry Morgan in *Crossing to Safety.* Like these other first-person narrators, Palmer would seem to reflect a split in Stegner's own personality between detachment and involvement and the internal conflict that sometimes resulted. Finding a voice would seem to have come, at least in part, out of Stegner's ability to cast this split in his own life and personality into fictional form.

While the narrators in the novels who would evolve out of Palmer all have a romantic streak, Palmer's romanticism is so extreme that it carries him into fundamentally misjudging the people he observes. In the story he looks out his study window at the women who line up along the wall every day, navy wives who during World War II wait at their mailboxes for word of their husbands, and out of his bookishness he is reminded of Homer's Penelope "on the rocky isle of Ithaca above the wine-dark sea," and he finds himself getting "a little sentimental about these women" (42). Of course, the point of the story depends on the unreliability of his perceptual frame-work—the women turn out, on closer acquaintance, to be very unromantic figures indeed. One of his Penelopes turns out to be a dope addict; another smothers her child with overprotectiveness; another is filled with "cold hos-tility"; another, unmarried, has become pregnant and worries that her lover may not come back and "make a decent woman" of her. They are backbiting, self-involved, and in conflict with one another—not at all the admirably placid, patient, heroic figures he has imagined them to be. It is in a sense, to return to Bakhtin, a story that within itself turns from the authoritarian voice to a dialogic conflict of several voices, as each woman in the end figuratively "insists" on establishing her own real identity.

To a lesser extent the narrators of the later novels, Joe Allston, Lyman Ward, and Larry Morgan, are unreliable in their perceptions, and they, too, want to place the people around them as players in their personally scripted dramas, dramas reflecting their preconceptions, prejudices, and desires. This tendency contributes to a larger theme that appears throughout Stegner's work, that of identity—our own (that is, that of the narrator or, in the case of "The Women on the Wall," the center of consciousness) and that of others (the characters observed by the narrator). Each novel carried by the first-person narrators mentioned above has as its central concern an effort to understand and make a judgment about a major character in the work, a pattern that is prefigured in "A Field Guide to the Western Birds." Each of these narrators finds himself in a position where he is not only unsure of precisely what judgment to make but also unsure about his own ability or qualifications to make any judgment. And the "dialogue," to use Bakhtin's term, in these novels is primarily concerned with a conflict between the narrator and one or more other characters about the nature or role of the ambiguous character who is both part of the discussion and the object of it.

Mr. Palmer, by contrast, seems so certain of his own vision that both he and the reader are shocked by his mistake, and the thought that sticks with us from "The Women on the Wall" is the complete failure of the center of consciousness to see things as they really are. Of course, as a bachelor Palmer does not have the wife who is always there to attempt to correct through dialogue the eyesight of narrator husbands Joe Allston and Larry Morgan. Ultimately, Palmer's fussiness and egocentricity alienate us, and his errors are so gross that we cannot trust or believe in him. Not so Joe Allston, whom we first encounter in the long short story "A Field Guide to the Western Birds."[4] Joe, even in his own time, was not a fashionable character—the late-middle-aged, white, upper-middle-class male in the sixties represented what was then referred to scornfully as "the establishment" and today has no credentials as a victim of either ethnic or gender discrimination to recommend him.

Nevertheless, he seems to represent a point of view, a tone, an approach to life, that is engaging, entertaining, and, above all, believable. The essence of the man that leads to our engagement is that he, like his creator, is a truth seeker. While Mr. Palmer blunders into truth and is somewhat sorry for it, Joe Allston holds out a stricter standard for himself and for others. Like Palmer, he makes judgments and is proven wrong, but his judgments do not come out of his romanticism or egotism; they come from better motives—out of his skeptical attempts to see behind appearances and his concern for the welfare of others. Unlike Mr. Palmer, Allston (and all his counterparts) is a learning character: he wants to engage in dialogue; the exchange of views is his lifeblood, whereas Palmer would rather keep to himself in order to keep his illusions. Mr. Palmer is not going to modify his viewpoint or beliefs, but Allston, even at sixty-six, is still wondering what the world is about and still making judgments while wondering if he is right. And typically, not only in this story but in the novels mentioned above, the narrator at any given moment may or may not be wrong. He is not quite sure and neither are we, and that is the beauty of it—Stegner is able by his characterizations to convey a sense of the uncertainty of life; and through the ongoing external and internal dialogues, we are given evidence once again that life is an ambiguous proposition at best. Stegner's voices here provide ample opportunity for complex perceptions that can be variously interpreted.

IV

Retired from a career as a literary agent in New York to a California suburb, Joe Allston spends much of his time looking out his study window, bird watching, rather than writing his memoirs. This bird watching is a complicated metaphor that stretches on from the story into the two novels that also use Allston as narrator. First of all, of course, there is the declaration in the metaphor that this character is, above all, an observer. He looks out, away from himself, giving up the more self-centered occupation of writing memoirs, explaining with some irony at one point in the story, "I am beginning to understand the temptation to be literary and indulge the senses. It is a full-time job just watching and listening here" (313).

Second, his watching involves identification and classification, a process that extends from real birds to those "western birds," that is, the people he encounters in his neighborhood and at social gatherings. At the party that takes up most of the story, he looks at the various guests and thinks, "It is all out of some bird book, how the species cling together, and the juncoes and the linnets and the seedeaters hop around in one place, and the robins raid the toyon berries *en masse*, and the jaybirds yak away together in the almond trees" (332). His story is a modified version of Mr. Palmer's story in that despite long experience with various kinds of people, he learns, in the case of the guest of honor, that classifying people is not always so certain or so easy as classifying birds.

Joe and his wife, Ruth, have been invited by neighbors Bill and Sue Casement to a concert-party—cocktails, a gourmet catered dinner, and afterward, outside near the pool, a recital by a down-on-his-luck young pianist named Kaminski. Kaminski turns out to be an arrogant and unhappy artist who does his best to insult everyone and to make Sue Casement, his benefactress, as uncomfortable as possible. At one point, the pianist throws a

tantrum about the guests' eating and drinking so much before the performance. Standing in the buffet line, Joe and Ruth see Kaminski stalk off, apparently threatening not to play, pursued by Sue, and Ruth comments:

> "If she weren't so nice it would be almost funny."
>
> "But she *is* so nice."
>
> "Yes," she says. "Poor Sue."
>
> As I circle my nose above the heaped and delectable trencher, the
> thought of Kaminski's bald scorn of food and drink boils over in my
> insides. Is he opposed to nourishment? "A pituitary monster," I say,
> "straight out of Dostoevsky."
>
> "Your distaste was a little obvious."
>
> "I can't help it. He curdled my adrenal glands."
>
> "You make everything so endocrine," she says. "He wasn't that bad. In
> fact, he had a point. It *is* a little alcoholic for a musicale."
>
> "It's the only kind of party they know how to give."
>
> "But it still isn't quite the best way to show off a pianist."
>
> "All right," I say. "Suppose you're right. Is it his proper place to act as
> if he'd been captured and dragged here? He's the beneficiary, after all."
>
> "I expect he has to humiliate her," Ruth says.
>
> Sometimes she can surprise me. I remark that without an M.D. she is
> not entitled to practice psychiatry. So maybe he does have to humiliate
> her. That is exactly one of the seven thousand two hundred and fourteen
> things in him that irritate the hell out of me.
>
> "But it'll be ghastly," says Ruth in her whisper, "if she can't manage to
> get him to play."
>
> I address myself to the trencher. . . . But Ruth's remark of a minute
> before continues to go around in me like an auger, and I burst out again:
> "Humiliate her, uh? How to achieve power. . . . Did it ever strike you
> how much attention a difficult cross-grained bastard gets, just by being
> difficult?" (329–30)

Here, unlike in Stegner's early fiction, often so flat, the dialogue crackles
and snaps like a free wire dangling from a power pole. The wire vibrates
between positive and negative electrical charges, as if the narrator has been
split into male and female, a common phenomenon in these later novels,
giving them all Bakhtin's "polyphonic" quality. Lyman Ward in *Angle of*

Repose, for example, takes his own part but also the part of his grand-mother, whom he recreates from her letters. This, by the way, is mirrored in Stegner's own use of the letters of a real-life woman, Mary Hallock Foote, as basis for dividing himself to create the dialogic conflict of the novel. The electricity metaphor is apropos in that one of the main things that Stegner achieves through this voice—divided or undivided— is interest. Joe—not to mention his wife—is intelligent, intensely observant, and above all, witty. The power of the personalities of these late narrators—Lyman Ward and Larry Morgan, as well as Joe—and their interaction with their female coun-terparts force us to read on.

Although Joe, as we have just seen, takes an immediate dislike to this "Glandular Genius," as he calls Kaminski, he also begins to feel somewhat uncomfortable himself at the surfeit of food and drink on "this movie set where the standard of everything is excess" (334). The contradiction inherent in his objection to Kaminski's saying pretty much the same thing underlines the ambiguity of Allston's position—he is both right and wrong in his reac-tions to the pianist. Once again the narrator is split, the split reflecting the author's own ambiguity and authoritarian control. But there is also a fore-shadowing in Joe's feeling of discomfort at the surfeit of the party, a fore-shadowing of the reversal of the ending, a hint that the condescension of the wealthy, as well-intentioned as they may be, toward the artist is at the root of the conflict. It is a conflict that Joe feels but initially misunderstands. Another thing that Stegner achieves with the adoption of the Joe Allston voice is a narrator so complex in himself that the author is able to extend the dimensions of his narrative.

As the performance begins, Joe listens carefully in order to hear how good a pianist Kaminski is, but typically, Joe backtracks mentally, wondering if, after all, he is capable of any final judgment:

God spare me from ever being called a critic, or even a judge of music—even a listener. Like most people, I think I can tell a dub from a compe-tent hand, and it is plain at once that Kaminski is competent. The shades of competence are another thing. They are where the Soul comes in, and I look with suspicion on those who wear their souls outside. I am not capable in any case of judging Kaminski's soul. Maybe it is such a soul as swoons into the world only once in a hundred years. Maybe, again, it is such a G.G. [Glandular Genius] soul as I have seen on Madison Avenue and elsewhere in my time. (336)

Later, Allston almost gloats when he thinks he hears "a butch, a fat naked, staring discord" (338) during Kaminski's performance of a difficult Bach piece. Here, as elsewhere throughout the story, Allston shows himself to be, if not expert, certainly very knowledgeable about music, once again contradicting himself and showing the difference between how he chooses to present himself to the reader—the modest appreciator of music—and the acute critic he actually is. The reader, who by now shares Allston's dislike of Kaminski, finds the pianist's disintegration after the recital almost predictable, almost enjoyable. In genteel terms, Kaminski turns out to be a thoroughly despicable case: in a long drunken public confession he proclaims his need to fail and his fraudulent identity as a Polish Jew victimized by the Nazis. Finally, when the host tries to pull him off to bed, he staggers into a chair and then falls into the pool. The harmony, the "niceness," as it might better be called in this upper-middle-class atmosphere, of the occasion has been thoroughly shattered.

But things are not as they seem. As Joe and Ruth drive home, Joe discovers that Ruth, whose judgment in such matters he respects more than his own, thinks that Kaminski is, indeed, very good, exceptional—worth helping toward a concert in New York. But, of course, this chance, which might have been his only chance, is now gone. Joe wonders, "Why would he? . . . Where in God's name does he belong?" and "How shall a nest of robins deal with a cuckoo chick? And how should a cuckoo chick, which has no natural home except the one he usurps, behave himself in a robin's nest? And what if the cuckoo is sensitive, or Spiritual, or insecure? Christ" (358). The epiphany is ambiguous—the moral escapes him, and life remains as obscure as the fog that they drive through on the way back from the party. All Joe can do is be grateful to Ruth "for the forty years during which she has stood between me and myself" (359).

A complicated narrator—a fallible wise man, as I might call him—has led us down the garden path into a complex of emotions difficult for the reader to sort out. It is a pattern repeated over and over again in these final novels. Kaminski is brimming over with self-pity; he is a phony, a pretender; he is arrogant and cruel and filled with self-importance—so that Joe Allston's dislike, and ours, are certainly justified. But Kaminski is also a poor Jewish young man, with a very real talent, thrust into a scene of up-scale opulence dominated by a wealthy society that is with few exceptions largely populated by pretenders and Philistines: the entire party is a kind of charade of artistic appreciation. Are not the artist's discomfort, posturing, and anger justified? Just because he makes a social stink, are we justified in hating him, gloating over his downfall? In the shadow of this reversal, think too of the complications in relationship and of judgment presented by Lyman Ward's grandmother, by Joe Allston's Marian in *All the Little Live Things,* and of Larry Morgan's Charity.

Even Joe Allston, who knows something about art and music, is wrong and comes to admit it, realizing that the identification of the human species can be a lot more difficult and fraught with possible error than he earlier in the story thinks it to be. At the end, the narrator is mired in doubt: "I don't know whether I'm tired, or sad, or confused. Or maybe just irritated that they don't give you enough time in a single life to figure anything out" (359). If there is a lesson, it is not so much about the nature of life as it is about the processes of observing and judging others, processes that need to be performed with humility and openness, with conclusions always subject to revision.

∨

Such is the nature of this narrator as he evolved through these stories to become the voice, the fallible wise man of the later novels. Stegner remarked that "Any work of art is the product of a total human being," but it is only with these late works that he was able to bring himself totally to his art (*On the Teaching* 22). Stegner was fond of quoting Robert Frost as saying that "a fiction writer should be able to tell what happened to himself as if it has happened to someone else, and what happened to someone else as if it had happened to himself" (24). At the beginning of his career, with such works as *On a Darkling Plain,* Stegner tended to reverse Frost's admonition by telling what happened to someone else as if it had indeed happened to someone else—giving distance to those things which were in fact distant. During his period of autobiographical fiction, in *The Big Rock Candy Mountain* and the stories that led up to it, he was able to make a correction, at least temporarily, bringing weight to his own story by giving it distance.

But it was only with the evolution of the Joe Allston voice and stance that Stegner was able to create a narrator who is a fiction, someone other than himself, and yet bring to that fiction all his faculties, all the force of his personality. That which is distant—the fictional personality—is made near and real; and through the author's investment of himself, his deep participation, the complexities and ambiguities of living are made manifest. In these late novels Stegner was able, to go back to Albert J. Guerard's description of the "personal voice," to achieve "a voice that is the intimate and often unconscious expression of his temperament and unborrowed personality, a voice that in its structures and rhythms reflects the way his mind moves" (136). More than that, Stegner was able to divide that voice into roles that engage in this dialogue that is the substance of these works, roles that reflect his own splits into male and female, detached and involved, accurate and inaccurate in perception. It was a mark of his maturity as a writer that in the later part of his career he accomplished such a complex division and then synthesis.

The voices of his primary narrators make use of Wallace Stegner's personal assets: his dry sense of humor and wit (which make these later novels so entertaining); his willingness to laugh at himself and to examine himself; his skepticism; his openness to learning; his search for the truths behind cultural and historical myth; his concern for the preservation of the earth. Over time the narrators get closer and closer to the inner man, his concerns and values, as the man sheds his reluctance to risk and reveal himself—and divide himself to reveal his own uncertainties. The narrators are supercharged by the author's investment but remain fictions.

The achievement of this voice, is, as we might call it, the Jamesian solution, although James did not adopt the first-person point of view. It is that step beyond autobiographical achievement—to bring an "other" voice fully to life. Perhaps it is no coincidence, then, that Stegner followed James in a pattern of lifelong growth, creating his greatest work near the end of his career. During a seminar at Dartmouth College, Stegner commented on the possibility of such growth:

> Largeness is a lifelong matter—sometimes a conscious goal, sometimes not. You enlarge yourself because that is the kind of individual you are. You grow because you are not content *not* to. You are like a beaver that chews constantly because if it doesn't, its teeth grow long and lock. . . .

> If you are a grower and a writer as well, your writing should get better
> and larger and wiser. (*On the Teaching* 38)

His growth came as a result of being able to give up the authoritarian control of the early novels, and he enlarged himself by instead creating characters who are "free people," people, in Bakhtin's words, "who are capable of
standing beside their creator, of disagreeing with him, and even rebelling
against him" (4).

As he grew older, Stegner began to think he had grown wiser, but during
the last two decades of his life, he tended toward discarding that notion,
wondering at times if he had gained any wisdom at all. His later storytellers
seem to reflect this growing doubt. But one of the things that draws us most
to them—Joe Allston, Lyman Ward, and Larry Morgan—is that their wisdom is certified by their fallibility, their uncertainty. All of them, even at a
late stage of life, are learning and growing, and although they have strong
values and carefully nurtured, strong personalities, they nevertheless remain
open to experience. In this they reflect their creator who, until he died from
injuries in an auto accident at eighty-four, was active, curious, who was
reading, writing, traveling, and giving speeches. Throughout his last decades,
Stegner gave himself almost entirely to his art and to his life as a writer,
investing his knowledge and experience, as well as his doubts, in those ventriloquist dummies, as he called them, who spoke for him.

CHAPTER SEVEN

The Short Stories
The College Years

Like many writers of fiction, Wallace Stegner began his career by writing short stories. His first publication came in 1930 with the story "Blood Stain" in *Pen,* the literary magazine at the University of Utah. His career as a professional did not begin until 1937, however, when he published the novelette *Remembering Laughter* in *Redbook.* He went on from this prize-winning novelette to a career as a writer of both short stories and novels, although he achieved more success, early on, with his stories.

As a story writer he had two bursts of activity: from 1938 to 1943, when he published eighteen stories, and from 1947 to 1958, when he published fifteen. It was not until 1943, several years after he had made his mark as a story writer, that he had his first success with a full-length novel, *The Big Rock Candy Mountain.* All in all, he published fifty-eight stories, most of them in quality, middlebrow magazines such as *Atlantic* and *Harper's,* and then ended his career as short fiction writer with the publication of "Carrion Spring" in *Esquire* in 1962. During two decades and a half he won five O. Henry Awards and had stories included in the *Best American Short Stories* series seven times. His stories were frequently anthologized and reprinted both in general collections and in textbooks for schools and colleges. Throughout his career, like many other writers, he wrote short fictions that either turned into novels or that contributed elements to a longer work. He often solved technical problems by working with the short form, finding solutions that he then carried over into his novels (as I have described in "Finding a Voice of His Own" in this volume).

In 1990, three years before his death, most of Stegner's stories were republished in *Collected Stories of Wallace Stegner*. Anne Tyler, in her review of this collection in the *New York Times Book Review* (March 18, 1990, 18), wrote that even though, as Stegner explained in his foreword, he had given up the short form some years earlier,

> His admirers will take him any way they can get him—novels, essays, biographies—but after sinking into these stories gathered from "a lifetime of writing," we can't help but mourn the passing of his short story days. These stories are so large; they're so whole hearted. Plainly, he never set out to write a *mere* short story. It was all or nothing.

What characterizes Stegner's short fiction is that it has little overt action and depends instead on evolving psychological states—perceptions of oneself and of others, situations or environments that generate emotions and quiet realizations. In the quiet, slowly developing power of his stories we feel the influence of the writer he admired most, Anton Chekhov. On one occasion, explaining what he had learned from the Russian writer, he said, "Chekhov had a way of turning up the rheostat, little by little. . . . Joyce called it an epiphany. Katherine Mansfield called it a nuance" (Shenker n. pag.).

Two other writers Stegner particularly admired were Joseph Conrad, the first major literary figure whose work he had read as a youngster, and William Faulkner. Conrad provided an example to him, through the use of the narrator Marlowe, of the importance of point of view, an importance Stegner stressed over and over again to his creative writing students. Faulkner reinforced Stegner's own sense of the importance of history and led him to his own frequent experiments with the manipulation of time in his fiction: Faulkner had taught him that in literature one can represent the past and the present as all of one piece. We can see this bringing together of past and present in several of Stegner's stories, including the three that we will be looking at shortly: "Maiden in a Tower," "Beyond the Glass Mountain," and "The Blue-Winged Teal."

Because of his familiarity with the work of nearly all the major short-story writers of times past, as well as of his own time (he would also come to know many of them personally and invite them to lecture or teach in his creative writing program at Stanford), and after extensive experience of teaching story writing, Stegner would develop a flexible, inclusive view of the form. Late in life, at a reading on his book tour to publicize his *Collected Stories* (1990), he said, "I don't have any formula or theory of the short story. The only thing I do demand of a short story, my own or anyone else's, is that it ought to close some sort of circuit—a plot circuit, an emotional circuit, psychological circuit, a circuit of understanding, so in the end there is some sense of completion" (Kazak 29).

Most of Stegner's stories, while not explicitly autobiographical, can nevertheless be placed in regard to some period of his life—stories related to his childhood, to his adolescence, to his early teaching career, and so on. Three of his best stories can be connected to his college years, not because they were written in college but because they go back, either directly or by flashback, to that period: "Maiden in a Tower," "Beyond the Glass Mountain," and "The Blue-Winged Teal." Stegner went for three and a half years to the University of Utah in Salt Lake City (1927–30), getting his degree and then taking a fellowship at the University of Iowa, where he got both his master's and his doctorate (1930–35).

The first of these stories, "Maiden in a Tower," takes the narrator back to his senior year at the University of Utah. In those days the university existed in a comfortable haze of self-satisfied provinciality—three thousand clean-cut students watched over by the elders of the Mormon Church. In looking back on his years there, Stegner recalled having mixed emotions about the university. On the one hand, he found the experience a good one "because that was the first chance any of us had to see minds at work at all. They weren't great minds, but they were at work, and I think there was a lot of good teaching that went on. . . . My teachers were very kind to me, and they opened up a lot of doors."[1]

On the other hand, the atmosphere of the school was to some extent smothered by the intellectual limitations that were applied by the church, something that Stegner became more and more conscious of as he got older. In his late teens, he was tall, lanky, bespectacled, and handsome; he was an intellectual, but also played varsity tennis. He had a part-time job throughout and paid most of his school expenses, but also was a fraternity man, liked to party, and was a hit with young women. He had an enormous amount of energy. Much of his wilder activity was motivated by a spirit of rebellion, rebellion against the atmosphere of the school and the small-town provinciality of Salt Lake.

He was encouraged to strike out intellectually and socially by one of his teachers during his freshman year, Vardis Fisher. The Idaho poet and novelist was, in Stegner's words, "one of those teachers who liked to take can openers to unopened minds," with the premise that his students had never seen anything in their sheltered lives and that a real idea would shock the pants off of them (Stegner and Etulain 25). During Wallace's last two years at the University of Utah, 1928–1930, a woman friend by the name of Peg Foster took over the shepherding of his rebellion where Fisher left off. Attractive, in her early twenties, and living off-campus in an apartment, Foster ran a literary salon for the brighter young professors of English literature and their most promising students. Wallace recalls that despite the airless quality of the university,

> I don't think we all felt starved for culture. I don't think we had any capacity for culture. That's where . . . Peg Foster came in because she wrote poetry and she knew a lot of poetry. It was kind of nice, off the university grounds as it were, to run into somebody who took poetry seriously.[2]

Another close friend, Red Cowan, who was on the tennis team and also had a job at the flooring store where Wallace worked all during his college years, remembers Foster as a "rather exotic creature" who wore slinky dresses, figured shawls, and dangling earrings. Like the student group that surrounded Vardis Fisher, Peg Foster's friends loved to poke fun at what they considered narrow-minded, bourgeois Salt Lake.

One of a series of stories that deal with Stegner's late college years, "Maiden in a Tower," features a character modeled after Foster. Just as in his novel *Recapitulation*, "Maiden in a Tower" (1954) is told in retrospect, by an older man whose memory has been jogged by returning to Salt Lake. As in a number of Stegner stories dealing with childhood and adolescence, we have a story with an innocuous surface but a threatening undertow. But whereas in the stories of early life it is the pain of not belonging that underlies the experiences, here it is the pain of regret in the mature adult for the failure to act in his youth.

Kimball Harris is the man who takes a journey in memory back twenty-five years to a Bohemian life in the salon of the beautiful Holly. The journey starts in the present, when he returns in order to make arrangements for the burial of what was his last living close relative, Aunt Margaret, "never very lovable, never dear to him" ("Maiden" 271). Even as he drives into the city, he finds himself "alert with the odd notion that he was returning both through distance and through time" (268). And when, after looking up the address in the phone book in his hotel room, he finds that the funeral parlor might be located in what had been the house, broken up into apartments, in which Holly had lived, the memories began to flood back:

> Painters of bile-green landscapes, . . . makers of cherished prose, dream-tellers, correspondence-school psychoanalysts, they had swarmed through Holly's apartment and eddied around her queenly shape with noises like breaking china. He remembered her in her gold gown, a Proserpine or Circe. For an instant she was slim and tall in his mind and he saw her laughing in the midst of the excitement she created, and how her hair was smooth black and her eyes very dark blue and how she wore massive gold hoops in her ears. (269)

After going to the address and recognizing the house with its three-story stone tower, he is greeted by the mortician, and they conclude the burial arrangements for his aunt. On impulse he asks if he might see what had been Holly's third-floor apartment; he is given permission but warned that there is a woman's body there, dressed, but laid out in preparation for burial. The woman is a stranger, but the room, almost empty, is dominated by her presence. A Navajo squash-blossom necklace stands out in almost shocking contrast to her nondescript appearance and simple black dress. She becomes for Harris a talisman, not so much for specific memories as for his emotions in response to all that comes back to him. The bright, blooming necklace against the dark dress seems to suggest a giving-over to the joy of life: "What it said of frivolity, girlishness, love of ornament and of gaiety and of life made him like her," but "the way it lay on the sober black crepe breast preached the saddest lesson he had ever learned" (278).

What that lesson might be is not given to us explicitly. But what we do know from the story is that at a crucial moment in his life he failed to embrace life, failed to take the risk. Holly is not only beautiful, provocative, the center of attention, the girl every man around her was in love with, but also a risk-taker, a generator of excitement. Typical of her is her plan for the miniature golf course across the street: she would fill the water holes with crocodiles, sow the sandtraps with sidewinders, and "hide a black widow spider in every hole so that holing out and picking up your ball would earn you some excitement" (274). Harris remembers, "Live it dangerously. It was strange to recall how essential that had seemed" (274).

However, there is a play-acting quality to the salon, everyone taking on a Bohemian-prescribed role in reaction to the safe, sane—and dull—surroundings of the Mormon city. In retrospect, Harris realizes that "under the sheath [Holly] was positively virginal; if you cracked the enamel of her sophistication you found a delighted little girl playing life" (275). Their relationship has been a flirtatious game so ingrained in him that one day, near the end of Holly's reign in the apartment, when life suddenly becomes real, he is unable to respond to the challenge, "to live dangerously." Pressing against him and crying, she begs him, "Kim, Kim, get me out of here! I want to get out of this. This is all no good, I've got to, Kim, please!" (276).

But Harris has played the game of make-believe emotion too long and retreats into mock consolation, patting her on the head. He finds the memory of this moment of immaturity and timidity humiliating. Although from "a life of prudence" he has gotten a wife and children he cares for deeply, it seems to him, as he stands there in that room in the mortuary remembering Holly, that "his failure to take her when she offered herself was one of the saddest failures of his life" (277). It is a memory that he has repressed, and coming back under these circumstances fills him with regret. Or, to frame the moment in terms of the Robert Frost poem, it was a place where the road divided and he took the one most traveled by, the one most comfortable. As he leaves the room and the dead body there, he hears almost in panic "the four quick raps his heels made on the bare floor before they found the consoling softness of the stairs" (278)—perhaps he has heard "Time's wingèd chariot," or maybe the person he used to be is dogging his heels.

The story is an investigation into safety and risk, life and death, ongoing experience and memory. It emphasizes the importance of the quality of life, the need to embrace life totally and take the chance. As in so much of Stegner's fiction, especially his later work, the past and present are mixed together to become all of one piece, so that the present derives its meaning from the past and the past defines our identity. We see this use of time in several of the stories but more obviously in novels such as *Recapitulation*, *Angle of Repose*, and *Crossing to Safety*. Stegner made a conscious effort in his fiction to, in his words, "interpenetrate the past and present," and in several places he stated his goal to do for the West what Faulkner had done for Mississippi, to discover "a usable continuity between the past and present" ("Born a Square" 179). Of course, it was an effort that demonstrated itself in much of his fiction, whether set in the West or not. Another of the stories that intermixes memories with present experience and like "Maiden in a Tower" goes back in its recollections to the central character's college days is "Beyond the Glass Mountain" (1947).

Although both stories are about memory, its place in "Beyond the Glass Mountain" is not so much about regret for actions not taken as about nostalgia—the sentimentalizing of the past, which is then seen to be in conflict with reality. We are also involved here with the conflicting perspectives of different times and different people. Do people change so much over time that we can no longer reach them? Can we ever really say that we know another person? Understand their situation? The main character, Mark Aker, has become an Easterner and is a success, a well-known and well-traveled scientist. In a trip back to his undergraduate university (Iowa, where Stegner went to graduate school), like Kimball Harris in "Maiden" he finds himself trying to recover the feelings of his past:

> Odd compulsions moved him. He found himself reciting the names of all the main university buildings. . . . Mark looked curiously at the few students he met, wondering if they felt as he felt the charm and warmth that lay in the brick streets and the sleepy river and the sun-warmed brick and stone of the university. . . .
>
> All of it was still there—unimaginably varied smells and sounds and sights that together made up the way he had once lived, the thing he had once been, perhaps the thing he still was. (23–24)

But as in so many of his stories, Stegner sets up the reader for a reversal through his use of the center of consciousness point of view. We are led to identify with Mark Aker—a straight shooter who wants only to be helpful, to share his warm response to the past, and, most of all, to share his expectations in regard to renewing his friendship with his old roommate, Mel. Then

Stegner sets out to undermine that warm feeling and those expectations by dropping bits and pieces of information that, first, plant a seed of unease in our minds and, then, make it grow until it becomes distress.

Mark is grateful to Mel for all he did for him during their undergraduate days. He had looked up to him as a model, a gracious, sharing person who had taught their whole group some important values. But as Mark went on to success, Mel was left behind in a bad marriage and a confining job in Iowa City. In college Mel had put on a drunk act that, along with calling Mark "Canby" (for some unknown reason), became a running joke between them. Over the years Mel's drunk act made it impossible for Mark to communicate anything directly to him over the telephone, but Mark felt that behind the act, Mel was reaching out for help of some kind. Now, on his return to Iowa City, Mark telephones Mel and is baffled when Mel takes up his routine again and goes on and on with it. Is he simply taking the joke too far, or has he become permanently a drunk, a caricature of himself?

At Mel's house, Mark renews acquaintance with Mel's wife, Tamsen, who "had always been shrewd, and . . . had been all her life one of the world's most accomplished and convincing liars" (27). In college she had slept around and, more recently, she and Mel had nearly divorced as a result of her affair with a golf pro.

Now she seems to encourage her husband's drinking. As Mark's visit continues, it becomes clear that the underlying atmosphere of the house is poisonous, while on the surface they keep up the charade of a jovial reunion. Late in the story, Mark can only tell Mel what he wants to tell him in his mind:

> For the love of God, get that divorce, for the sake of the boy and for your own sake. She'll suck you dry like an old orange skin. You're already so far gone I could cry—soggy with alcohol and with that comedy-routine front on all the time. Come and stay with me, I'll line you up with Alcoholics Anonymous if you want. Give me a chance to pay some of what I owe you. (28)

But, he realizes, "You simply did not say things like that."

At the end of his visit, Mark makes one last, lame attempt to break through his friend's defenses, gripping his hand and looking into his eyes, telling him that he wishes him the best and starts to offer, in general terms, his help. But he stops. "Mel was looking at him without any of the sodden fuzziness that had marked him for the past hour. His eyes were pained, intent, sad. On his delicate bruised lips there was a flicker of derision" (31). In those last words, "a flicker of derision," the story seems to deconstruct and fall to pieces at the bottom of our minds. What are we to make of this? Right before this ending, as the two men take leave of Tamsen at the door (Mel will walk Mark to the corner), Mark is "trying to decide whether the look in her clear eyes had been triumphant, or whether there had actually been any look at all" (30). The sense one gets from this and other tidbits about Tamsen's influence on her husband is that she seems to be operating more or less as the evil corrupter and has been during Mark's visit in combat with him, the "rescuing angel," for Mel's soul. Do Mel's last words indicate that he is irretrievably lost, or that he is not lost at all but playing a game with everyone including his wife, or simply that he scorns what he perceives as Mark's superior attitude, his condescension, his pity? Has Mark's earlier relationship with Mel blinded him to his friend's real situation, or have his values, his successes, blinded him to his friend's chosen values and needs?

We can go back to a story about childhood, like "Two Rivers," and see some of the same questions being raised. Can two people really know each other—even a son and his mother? How do our past and memories of the past, with differing reactions to the same events, influence our present identities? One other story that brings together time, identity, and communication—or lack of it—and is set in the period of Stegner's graduate school years is "The Blue-Winged Teal" (1950), one of Stegner's best-known pieces. It too ends in a "situation revealed," revealed in puzzling ambiguity, raising more questions than it answers.

As much as any story that Stegner ever wrote, this is a story of atmosphere—an atmosphere that is dreary, shabby, and charged with barely suppressed hostility and despair. The story's setting, time and place, is patterned on a traumatic period in Stegner's own life when, after having graduated from the University of Utah (in 1930) and gone on to graduate school at the University of Iowa for two years, he was staying with his father in an apartment in Salt Lake City. His mother had just suffered a terrible death from cancer, and when her pain had become too severe, his father had fled the scene, leaving Wallace to care for his mother until her death. He never forgave his father and had come to hate him, not only for abandoning his wife during her crisis but for the outlaw pattern of living over the years that had isolated her and deprived the family of any kind of normal existence. While Wallace had been in graduate school, the banks had failed, taking all his savings, and having left school to take care of his mother, he was now stuck with and dependent on his father, a bitter pill to swallow, until a new semester started and he could resume his studies.

In the story the superficial circumstances are changed and the events and supporting characters are imagined, but the central emotion, the son's hatred for his father, remains patterned after the author's actual feelings. One might guess that the story was, among other things, an exorcism of emotions that Stegner had held for much of his life. The dominant scene in the story is a poolroom managed by the father—in real life Stegner's father was in between occupations, having sold his interest in a Reno gambling house. And in the story, father and son share a furnished room, which makes the situation for the son more claustrophobic and unbearable than their sharing an apartment.

Although the son is called Henry here, one could think of this work as the last of the Bruce stories, the stories based on Stegner's growing up. (Indeed, in the version of the story that appears in the novel *Recapitulation,* the son's name is Bruce and the father's name, instead of John Lederer, is George Mason.)[3] "The Blue-Winged Teal" can be seen as a coda to the father-son relationship at the heart of these stories. The son, now an adult, reflects back on the relationship, and in an epiphany near the end of the story, he finds himself having the disturbing suspicion that there may well be another side to the story of his father and that in judging his father so severely, he may have been at least in part mistaken.

At loose ends and at odds with his father and the world, Henry has, on an impulse he does not understand, borrowed his father's shotgun, waders, and car and has gone duck hunting. Standing in front of his father's poolhall and loaded down with nine ducks, he wonders whatever possessed him to go. In the description that follows, Stegner reverses that sense of space and naturalness in prairie or woods that he uses so often in other stories to define the condition of his protagonist. Henry's emotional condition, depressed and antagonistic, is revealed in the dark, enclosed, and shabby scene he anticipates he will encounter after descending the stairs from the street down into his father's poolhall:

> He would find, sour contrast with the bright sky and the wind of
> the tule marshes, the cavelike room with its back corners in darkness,
> would smell that smell compounded of steam heat and cue-chalk dust,
> of sodden butts in cuspidors, of coffee and meat and beer smells from
> the counter, of cigarette smoke so unaired that it darkened the walls.
> From anywhere back of the middle tables there would be the pervasive
> reek of toilet disinfectant. (232)

After entering, he slides the string of ducks off his shoulder and swings the ducks over onto the bar: "They landed solidly—offering or tribute or ransom or whatever they were" (233).

The story continues from this point by tracing the emotional swings of Henry in his relationship to his father. Like that of a man in prison—and he feels as if he is—whose mood may alternate between despair and hope, Henry's attitude toward his father alternates between hatred and disgust on the one hand and a reluctant movement toward some slight sympathy on the other. What really sticks in his craw, however, is his father's easy return to his old pre-marriage pattern of illegal activities (managing an establishment that provides gambling and alcohol) and, especially, his taking up with the red-haired woman who comes into the poolhall late at night and waits for him to close up, a situation that Henry considers an insult to his mother's memory.

The father is pleased that there are enough ducks to give them a "real old-fashioned feed" (235), and that, in turn, reminds him of good times in the past that he and his son have shared. But Henry is determined to hold on to his hatred and not be drawn into his father's nostalgia. He refuses to let the moment ease the strain between them: "He did not forgive his father the poolhall, or forget the way the old man had sprung back into the old pattern, as if his wife had been a jailer and he was now released" (235).

A climax to the story comes that night as Henry lies in bed in the furnished room, awakened by his father coming home late and undressing in the dark. While pretending to be asleep, Henry smells "the smells his father brought with him: wet wool, stale tobacco, liquor; and above all, more penetrating than any, spreading through the room and polluting everything there, the echo of cheap musky perfume" (237). The perfume drives him to rage at himself for the sympathy, as slight as it had been, that he had felt for his father earlier in the day.

In a reversal of Nick Adams's systematic procedure to keep himself awake in Hemingway's "Now I Lay Me," carefully fishing in his mind every hole in a remembered stream, Henry is able to block out his anger and lead himself into sleep by bringing into his mind a lit pool table. It is a deliberate, almost too obvious irony, yet successfully suggests Henry's internal battle to take control of his mind and to suppress his rage in response to the perfume. Mentally, he carefully racks up the balls, breaks them, and one after another lines up each shot and pockets the balls. He knows that eventually "nothing would remain in his mind but the *clean* green cloth traced with running color and bounded by *simple* problems" [my emphasis] and that sometime in the middle of an intricate shot, he will slide off into sleep (239). That is to say, "If only life could be so simple; if only we had such control over our lives when we are awake."

But then his feelings shift yet again. His anger leads him the next day to find the old friends that, for some reason he cannot fathom, he has been avoiding and borrow enough money to break out of his paralysis, get to the coast, and renew his life. He has been deliberately nursing his hatred, dwelling on those things that might most stimulate his anger, but now he seems willing to let go. With a sense of release, he returns to the poolhall to tell his father he is leaving, only to find that he has forgotten about the duck feed. During dinner at the counter in the poolhall, once again his father reflects on times gone by, and when he recalls the mother's hand-painted china, his son responds by sitting "stiffly, angry that his mother's name should even be mentioned between them in this murky hole" (244).

His father has tacked duck wings up on the mirror frame behind the bar: "'Blue-wing teal,' his father said. . . . 'Just the wings, like that. Awful pretty. She thought a teal was about the prettiest little duck there was'" (244). The teal and their feathers are seen in the story as soft, gentle, and beautiful— their fragility and beauty a reminder of a soft and loving woman who is gone and a family that has been broken. Pinned up on the wall, they become an emblem of what was tender between the father and mother, something that their son will never take part in. Self-centered in his own mourning, Henry focuses almost exclusively on his own feelings, not even recognizing the possibility that his father, in his own way, may have cared deeply about his wife.

After talking about his wife and how she responded to the beauty of the teal, John Lederer suddenly breaks apart, his eyes fill with tears, and he stumbles down the stairs and through the pool tables to the toilet in the back. His son, shocked by his father's anguished look before he ran, thinks:

> The hell with you, the look had said. The hell with you . . . my son Henry. The hell with your ignorance, whether you're stupid or whether you just don't know all you think you know. You don't know enough to kick dirt down a hole. You know nothing at all, you know less than nothing because you know things wrong. (245)

This moment of revelation tears away the foundations of the son's anger, leaving him empty, somewhat bewildered, and wondering "if there was anything more to his life, or his father's life, . . . or anyone's life, than playing the careful games that deadened you into sleep" (245–46).

Later, after having returned to his counter, John Lederer starts to clean up the dishes from their dinner. His son takes that moment to say what he has come to say— that he will be leaving town:

> But he did not say it in anger, or with the cold command of himself that he had imagined in advance. He said it like a cry, and with the feeling he might have had on letting go the hand of a friend too weak and too exhausted to cling any longer to their inadequate shared driftwood in a wide cold sea. (246).

This ambiguous metaphor that finishes the story, has, like so many Stegner endings, multiple suggestive meanings. One such, certainly, is that the son realizes that despite his father's seedy life, he did love his wife and the three of them did have a family, regardless of its flaws. Without the mother, the warm, loving center of their lives, they are now both cast adrift on the cold sea of life. And further, Henry seems to realize that of the two of them, he and his father, he is the strongest, least dependent, and best able to make a life for himself. He still clings to his driftwood on a frigid and barren sea, and his life would seem to hold minimal promise; but he will survive, whereas his father is clearly lost.

This step toward forgiveness was not taken in life by Stegner until old age, when his anger dissipated and sorrow took its place, long after his father took his own life. The fiction provides an occasion for insight and forgiveness that life did not provide. What may strike us most about "The Blue-Winged Teal" is how, once again, the field has been reversed, how we are seduced by the son's emotions surrounding his father, which seem so justified until we and the son discover how mistaken we are. The lesson seems to be how easily we are led to be judgmental, lacking charity, lacking empathy, and lacking insight into the emotional conditions of others. The path of Henry's emotions is even more complex than summarized here. The story is a masterpiece of counterpoint, overtone, suggestive imagery, and skillful employment of point of view.

Going back to Stegner's story, after returning to graduate school at the University of Iowa in 1934, accompanied by his longtime friend Red Cowan, Stegner found his circumstances changed in several ways. He had obtained his master's by writing three short stories for his thesis, but his graduate advisor, Norman Foerster, suggested to him that he would have a hard time getting a college teaching job with a master's in creative writing and advised him to pursue a doctorate in American literature. Wallace found himself in a highly structured and demanding academic program, feeling totally inadequate to the task. Through the good offices of his former roommate, Wilbur Schramm, he was able to find a temporary job—teaching four classes for half-time pay at a small Lutheran school, Augustana College at Rock Island, Illinois. On Thursday evenings after classes were over, he would hitchhike the fifty miles to Iowa City, where he studied for his doctoral exams over the weekend.

Wilbur Schramm also introduced Wallace to his future wife, Mary Page. A graduate student in English who worked in the university library, Mary was delighted to meet and go out on a blind date with Wilbur's friend. She had read the stories that Wallace had written for his master's degree and was impressed by them. She was very attractive—pixie-like, so small and young looking that on at least one occasion she was mistaken for Wallace's daughter when they were together. Because she was well-read and intellectual, she and Wallace had a great deal in common, and he fell deeply in love with her. During the three-day weekends Wallace had at the university, they spent as much time together as he could spare from his studies, and usually, since he had little money, they spent their time just walking and talking. While he was at Augustana during the week, he wrote letter after letter to her, even though his letters might arrive in Iowa City after he did. It would seem that it was Wallace's stories that led Mary to fall in love with him, and it was his letters that clinched their relationship. All in all, this is good news for aspiring writers.

....

CHAPTER EIGHT

A Friendship with Consequences
Robert Frost and Wallace Stegner

The influence of one writer on another is a common story, but many writers either hide or deny such influence on their work as a matter of course. They do not want their work to be thought of as in any way derived or secondary; and protective of their claim to originality, they prefer to hide, if by nothing more than their silence, the influence of other writers who have inspired or guided them. But perhaps because he had only a modest ego, Wallace Stegner made no secret of the important influence Robert Frost's poetry had on his fiction, his life, and his thought. Indeed, by giving titles drawn from that poetry to two of his books, *Fire and Ice* and *Crossing to Safety*, he would seem to have advertised it. Writers are often influenced by the example of other writers long dead, but these two knew each other. The story here is one of a friendship, a relationship similar to that between father and son; the older man set an example of achievement for the ambitious, younger artist and stimulated his thinking, and the younger gave back admiration and companionship to the wounded and often unhappy poet. They would come to share a community of values and perceptions that would bring themes, images, and even language we associate with Frost to Wallace Stegner's fiction, often giving that fiction more depth and power.

We should note in passing that Stegner was not just a writer but also a teacher of American literature who was familiar with Frost's poetry long before they met. It is also important to note that the novelist was very fond of poetry, and from childhood on, he found pleasure in memorizing verse of all kinds. Although Stegner was a writer of fiction, he had the attraction to and memory for words, their sounds and evocative properties, that we think of as usually characterizing the poet. One of the games that he played with successive roommates in graduate school at Iowa consisted of starting a verse and then challenging the opponent to finish it.[1] Many of the verses he was attracted to stuck in his mind and became part of his way of seeing and saying things, but because he knew and admired Frost, that poetry assumed a particularly prominent place in his consciousness.

Of the many themes and perceptions Stegner and Frost shared, what stands out is an emphasis throughout their works on humankind's relationship to nature and on an underlayment of the mysterious and sometimes threatening in nature, which in turn reflects the unknown and sometimes sinister depths of human nature. Both were "country people" who took their ways of looking at things out of America's rural tradition of an intimate connection with the earth, of self-reliance, acceptance without complaint, and making do. Both men showed an awareness of the complexity of emotion that can stand between man and woman, and both had an admiration for those special qualities often displayed by womankind—compassion, concern for others, and willingness to sacrifice. Both the fiction writer and poet were tough-minded and realistic in their appraisal of life's potential fortunes and misfortunes, and both dealt extensively with such discomforting themes as loneliness, fear, aging, and death. But while Stegner was drawn to Frost's language and themes, the younger man felt free, as in most father-son relationships, to embrace some of the older man's ideas and rebel against and reject others. He was careful to grab hold of the positive, that which would help him grow, and let go of the negative—and there was a certain amount of the latter in Frost's makeup.

Stegner first met Frost at the Bread Loaf Writers' Conference in Vermont during the summer of 1938. His appointment to the faculty at the last moment had come as a result of recommendations to the director, Theodore Morrison, and the sudden withdrawal of one of the instructors. Stegner was flattered, but even though he had won a prize for his first novel and had a respectable publication record in both fiction and scholarship, he was younger, at twenty-nine, than nearly all the others and felt that he might well be in over his head among far more accomplished writers than he. Among those who were on the staff or were guest speakers that year were Gorham Munson, Bernard DeVoto, Helen Everitt, Fletcher Pratt, Archibald MacLeish, and Louis Untermeyer. The star, of course, was Robert Frost (Morrison 99).[2]

In person, Frost could be witty, funny, and even profound, but he was moody and a terrible egomaniac who could not stand to share the limelight with anyone else. Looking back on Frost in later years, Stegner testified to Frost's greatness and his fondness for him but also pointed to the Lawrence Thompson biography, which "demonstrates, in a hundred contexts, how much irritable self-love lay behind the rumpled white thatch and the rumpled clothes, behind the piercing blue eyes, back of the teasing smile" (DeVoto 204). At the same time, we need to remember the lack of regard he suffered for decades at the hands of most eastern establishment critics. Consider, for example, an incident that occurred during the time that Stegner was teaching at Harvard. He and Frost were sitting in an auditorium in Cambridge when a prominent eastern critic, rather late in the game, admitted that he had been wrong about Frost, who he now realized was not just a country bumpkin but rather a significant American poet. So angered by the condescension he found in this confession, Frost had to get up and leave the hall and even after leaving was so agitated that it was hours before his friend could calm him.[3]

The role of mentor or father figure suited his ego, and he cultivated that relationship with a number of younger men, Bernard DeVoto for several years and, beginning in the summer of 1938, Stegner. As a youngster just getting started, Stegner offered no challenge, and Frost took an immediate liking to this bright and obviously promising young man, who, in turn, was flattered by the attention of the great poet. It was Frost's habit to invite his young protégés

> to walk and talk and count stars with him along the midnight road to Middlebury Gap. More than one Fellow or junior staff member crawled into bed at two or three o'clock after such an expedition, his mind dizzy with the altitudes it had been in and every cell in his body convinced that Robert Frost was the wisest and sanest man alive. (DeVoto 205)

As one such junior staff member, Stegner could have been recording here his own reactions that summer, having accompanied the poet on several such walks.

But it was also that same summer when Stegner was made aware of the poet's darker side, which came out in the breakup of the relationship between Frost and DeVoto, a split that saddened Stegner, who had become fond of both men. Frost was pleased to have a writers' conference in his part of the country, rural Vermont, and looked upon Bread Loaf as his domain. Few poets could challenge his preeminence, but when Archibald MacLeish came to Bread Loaf as a visiting lecturer, Frost could not tolerate the devoted attention the other poet was receiving. As MacLeish read from his poetry, Frost sat in the back of the room folding and rolling some mimeographed notices in his hands. As the reading went on, to the obvious pleasure of the audience, the sound from the rattling papers became louder, more disturbing. Finally, unbelievably, Frost set a match to a pile of papers, and everyone's attention was diverted as he stomped out the flames and waved the smoke away.

Later, as MacLeish continued reading, Frost kept interrupting with a heckling commentary until DeVoto could not endure the baiting any more and burst out angrily, "For God's sake, Robert, let him read!" Stegner, who was there, did not see all that was happening, nor did he understand until later the implications of what he had seen. The conflict between these two strong personalities, which came to a head that evening, brought on a rift between Frost and DeVoto that was never healed, and at the end of the Bread Loaf session, DeVoto reportedly said to Frost while shaking his hand, "You're a good poet, Robert, but a bad man" (Stegner, *Robert Frost* 3; DeVoto 206–7)

Shaking his head at the vagaries of human nature, Stegner was inclined to agree, at least in regard to this specific incident once he had learned the details; but the greatness of the poetry, which had called forth such a deep response in him, and the stimulation he had found in Frost's company, seemed to overshadow any occasional display of pettiness. He was determined to try to maintain his friendship with both the poet and DeVoto.

Stegner would attend seven more Bread Loaf conferences, either on the staff or as guest speaker, and Frost was at most of these. And Stegner had further contact with Frost when, after that first summer in Vermont, he moved from teaching at the University of Wisconsin to Harvard. There, over six years, he was often in Frost's company, since during this time Frost was living first in Boston and then in Cambridge. They had a mutual friend in Ted Morrison, who was in charge of the writing program at Harvard; and

Morrison's wife, Kay, was Frost's secretary and "keeper," as the poet sometimes referred to her. It was common for Frost to show up, unannounced, at the Stegner house at dinnertime, and he and Stegner went to lectures and readings together on many evenings.

After going on to Stanford in 1945, Stegner repeatedly invited Frost to guest lecture as part of the creative writing program he headed, and Frost did come, finally, in 1958. Unfortunately, and much to Stegner's embarrassment, his old friend was snubbed by the head of the poetry component of the writing program, Yvor Winters, who had written a disparaging essay on Frost's poetry. Two years before his friend Frost died in 1963, Stegner wrote this tribute to him, defending him against his critics and against Winters's attack specifically:

> Of course this is a dark poet; any poet worth his salt is dark. But what one hears almost everywhere else in our literature, the accent of self-pity, one never hears in him. . . . He has a tough integrity like the weather, he knows that "earth's the right place for love,/I don't know where it's likely to go better." Far from being the "spiritual drifter" that one lamentably mistaken critic has called him, he persistently affirms, not in blindness to the world's pain, but in spite of it. He has always been out for stars, always had miles to go before he slept, never learned "how to be unhappy yet polite." ("Robert Frost" n. pag.)

At the end of his first summer at Bread Loaf in 1938, Wallace and his wife, Mary, retreated from the turmoil and hectic pace of the conference to the summer home of friends Peg and Phil Gray in nearby Greensboro, Vermont, on the shore of Caspian Lake. Phil Gray was a colleague at the University of Wisconsin, and he and his wife had become close friends of the Stegners and would remain so for the rest of their lives. (Many years later, after their deaths, Stegner would use the couple as the model for his central characters in *Crossing to Safety*.) The Grays had introduced the Stegners to Vermont, and they had fallen in love with it, ending up that summer buying an old farm—two hundred acres, with a dilapidated farmhouse and a broken-down barn—for six hundred dollars, most of the money coming from recent sales of stories to magazines. The barn was destroyed and the house damaged by the hurricane of 1938 that winter, but the Stegners were in the area to stay, returning nearly every summer for the rest of their lives (Kirgo 58).

Certainly the presence of the Grays increased the area's attraction, but it is also probable that Stegner's encounter with Frost at Bread Loaf, the author of all those Vermont poems that Stegner had taught and knew so well, gave the country for him a special glow. At graduate school at the University of Iowa, he had been immersed in Americana and by his graduate advisor, Norman Foerster, convinced of the importance for writers to explore all that was native to the American experience, and certainly there was nothing more "Americana" than Robert Frost's New England. Frost himself, Stegner said, was "as much in the American grain as Lincoln or Thoreau" ("Twilight" 221).

A close look at the stories and novels that Stegner wrote about Vermont reveals that it was difficult for him even to think about the area without Frost's language and themes coming to mind. Beyond that, although we may think of Stegner as essentially a western writer, what he found in Vermont seems to have taken the place of a West that was disappearing, or perhaps a West that never was. Here was a part of the country that was uncrowded, with room to walk and roam, with trees. There was so much moisture that you could not stop the trees and brush from growing, from replacing themselves rapidly after having been cut back. It was also a place that displayed the best of western virtues, a spirit of community and strong connection to the land. In speaking of Greensboro, he said, "Everybody who grows up here grows up working hard, and at all kinds of jobs. They're jacks-of-all-trades. They can fix things, toggle them up. That's characteristic of any frontier, and that's the kind of West that I grew up in" (Kirgo 59–60). In his later years, while he was becoming more and more pessimistic about the fate of the West under the pressures of population and exploitation, he felt that the old-fashioned insistence on hard work and integrity and the emphasis on personal responsibility he encountered in Vermont might very well save it from the population pressures that were beginning to threaten it ("The People" 184–85).

Tied together with these evaluative responses to the Vermont setting was Frost's reinforcement of many of the fiction writer's attitudes and perceptions. Frost was able to formulate and give intellectual authority to such values as individual effort and responsibility, which Stegner, out of his frontier past, already felt but had not at the beginning of their friendship fully articulated. But perhaps even more important to Stegner's writing, Frost seemed to imbue his protégé with an ironic stance in regard to human nature and a more tolerant, yet distanced view of human fallibility. Frost seems to have reinforced Stegner's own lack of sentimentality: as Stegner wrote in a tribute to his mentor, "The real jolt and force of Frost's love of life comes from the fact that it is cold at the root" ("Robert Frost" n. pag.). And Frost also seems to have further validated Stegner's tendency to find drama and meaningful conflict in ordinary lives.

Yet, when one speaks of values in particular, the weight of Frost's influence should be qualified. Stegner, even at a comparatively young age and even though somewhat awed by such stellar company, was still his own man, a person not easily influenced in directions contrary to his own basic beliefs. He did not, for example, let Frost's devotion to individualism persuade him when that devotion moved beyond a simple valuing of individual effort to become a sort of ultraconservative political doctrine. Stegner believed strongly in the importance of group effort and cooperation, and he supported the New Deal programs Frost scorned with such vehemence.

That glow, that sense, which both writers shared, of Vermont as a special place is reflected in "The Sweetness of the Twisted Apples," a story that more directly than most of Stegner's other fictions illustrates the extent to which Frost influenced his language and perceptions. Stegner wrote the story nearly ten years after he first met the poet, after he had an opportunity to become familiar with the Vermont countryside and its people firsthand. He and Mary often took off on walks or drove around in the car, exploring, more or less aimlessly, in an effort to learn about the area. The story is about just such a couple, also summer people, who drive down a track, hardly a road any more, on a voyage of discovery, although their ostensible purpose is to find suitable landscapes for the husband's painting. He is the artist, but it is his wife, Margaret, who is sensitive and open to experience. As they travel further and further away from the paved road, it seems as if they are also traveling back in time. Margaret spots an old stone wall that

within a few feet bent off to the right and was swallowed in impenetrable brush.

Margaret turned and stared back, but the wall did not appear again. It was lost in the woods, still carefully enclosing some obliterated and overgrown meadow, and all the labor that had built it was gone for the greater comfort of woodchucks and foxes. "It doesn't seem as if anything in America could be this old," she said. (222)

"It doesn't seem as if" is typical Frost syntax, and the passage as a whole, with its perception of nature reclaiming what humans have built, may remind us of Frost poems like "The Last Mowing," where the trees, in a shadowy march, threaten to take over a meadow that will no longer be mowed, or "The Wood-Pile," where vines and decay threaten to obliterate a cord of firewood left by someone in the woods. Both are traces of human-created order, like the wall spotted by the woman in the story, which will gradually fall and disappear in the inevitable processes of nature: "Something there is that doesn't love a wall," to cite another poem.

The couple go along the road and encounter a mother and daughter—strange country people isolated from the world, people who may remind us of such Frost characters as the mother and son in "The Witch of Coös," also isolated by place and time, whom he calls "two old believers." The daughter's, Sary's, sad tale of love lost in the passage of time is reminiscent of the recitation of love and youthful hope remembered by the woman in Frost's "The Pauper Witch of Grafton." But Sary's tale in the Stegner story is not just sad: Sary shows considerable day-to-day courage to endure despite her fate. The one beau that she had (she is gnome-like with a pinched face) dropped her to marry someone else and then came to live with his wife just down the road as Sary's only neighbors. Her equanimity in the face of what she calls "a disappointment," her unwillingness to whine or complain—these were traits that both Frost and Stegner admired.

Frost wrote a great deal about mutability, loneliness, old age, and the onset of death in such poems as "Provide, Provide," "An Old Man's Winter Night," and "After Apple-Picking." Wallace Stegner is one of the few major novelists and story writers of our time to adopt a similar perspective as a frequent theme in his work. While many of his contemporaries wrote about the artist, or some comparably sensitive figure, as a young man, Stegner often shows us the condition of the sensitive and perceptive older man or woman in novels such as *All the Little Live Things*, *The Spectator Bird*, and *Angle of Repose*.

In "An Old Man's Winter Night" Frost writes not only of the increasing isolation of the old but also, in a metaphor of a man closing up his farmhouse in preparation for going to bed, of the gradual dimming of his faculties:

> *What kept him from remembering what it was*
> *That brought him to that creaking room was age.*
> *He stood with barrels round him—at a loss.*
>
> . . . .
>
> *A light he was to no one but himself*
>
> . . . .
>
> *A quiet light, and then not even that.* (135)[4]

In Stegner's *The Spectator Bird*, Joe Allston has the realization that

> I really *am* getting old. It comes as a shock to realize that I am just killing time till time gets around to killing me. It is not arthritis and the other ailments. . . . It is just the general comprehension that nothing is building, everything is running down, there are no more chances for improvement. (89)

At another point in the novel, Stegner uses Joe Allston's thoughts of tooth decay as a synecdoche for the aging process:

> Last week . . . the dentist told me that the molar he has been trying to save by root canal work will have to go. I can read the future in that direction without cards or tea leaves. First a bridge, if he can find anything to hitch it to. Then a partial plate. Finally a complete cleaning out of old snags in preparation for false teeth, on television called dentures. There will be a morning when I look in the mirror and see an old sunken-cheeked stranger with scared eyes and a mouth like a sea urchin's. (11)

There is a another harshly realistic view of aging with a similar touch of black humor in Frost's "Provide, Provide," where the "once picture pride of Hollywood" is reduced to a scrub lady:

> *No memory of having starred*
> *Atones for later disregard,* (404)

The use of synecdoche was one of many lessons that Stegner learned from Frost. As far as the poet was concerned, "All an artist needs is samples" (Stegner and Etulain 161).

Both writers shared a deep sense of our mortality, our fragileness in the face of natural or social forces beyond our control, and the necessity to confront the inevitability of decay, neglect, and death—provide, provide. Neither Frost nor Stegner would endorse Rabbi Ben Ezra's enthusiasm for aging, "The best is yet to be." For them, as for Emily Dickinson, nature can be mysterious and often vaguely threatening to humans—dark, like the bottom of a well. In that connection we find that there is often in Stegner's fiction that sense of "haunting" so common to Frost's poetry. Again, the example can be taken from his story "The Sweetness of Twisted Apples." While her husband paints, the wife strolls up the road through a deserted village to a burying ground, where she stops and sits on a gravestone. She imagines the gradual abandonment of the area over the years: "There would be a day when you would come to your door and see nothing alive, hear no human sound, in your whole village" (226). Unlike her unseeing husband— ironically, the painter—she is attuned to the vibrations behind appearances: "She stood up uneasily. A hawk was methodically coursing the meadow beyond the graveyard. It was very still. She felt oppressed by the wide silent sky and afraid of the somehow threatening edge where meadow met woods, where not a leaf stirred but where something watched" (226). It is an apprehension familiar to Frost readers; we see it, among many places, in "The Fear," "Storm Fear," "An Old Man's Winter Night," and "The Hill Wife," poems in which something threatening lies just beyond the familiar, in which some tenor of the environment strikes apprehension or even terror in the heart of the sensitive observer.

Sometimes, as in the Stegner story, the threat in Frost is vague—just something out there in the darkness. In "An Old Man's Winter Night" the poem opens with "All out-of-doors looked darkly in at him" (135); the location of the threat is reversed in "The Hill Wife." When the couple in this poem return to their lonely farmhouse in the darkness, the threat may be inside:

They learned to rattle the lock and key
To give whatever might chance to be
Warning and time to be off in flight. (160)

But occasionally, the threat, the mysterious possible harm that may come out of nature, is objectified in the works of both the poet and the fiction writer.

In "The Hill Wife" the woman is haunted by a dark pine outside a window, which to her mind keeps "trying the window latch" of her bedroom; and in a recurring dream she fears "what the tree might do" (161). In "Storm Fear" an isolated farm family watches the snow, like an invading, implacable army, gradually covering everything outside, driven by a wind that "works against us in the dark" and

whispers with a sort of stifled bark,
The beast,
"Come out! Come out!—." (13).

This little vignette, this anti-Christmas-card snow scene, reminds us that no matter how removed we may think we are from the cave dweller surrounded by threatening beasts in the darkness beyond the fire, we are still vulnerable. The primitive is still with us, not only all around us but even within our own hearts, a response waiting to be struck. The farmer sees

How the cold creeps as the fire dies at length,—
How drifts are piled,

and he wonders

Whether 'tis in us to arise with day
And save ourselves unaided.(13)

Here, as in so many Frost poems, although the threat is ostensibly outside in nature, the subtext is that there is also something inside humankind itself that can under the right circumstance be brought back to the primitive. In some poems, that inner dimension of humans can itself be ominous. The mysterious and threatening outside, usually presented in the works of both writers as the dark and the cold, becomes emblematic of the inside. As Frost says in "Desert Places,"

They cannot scare me with their empty spaces
Between stars—on stars where no human race is.
I have it in me so much nearer home
To scare myself with my own desert places. (386)

There is perhaps nothing darker and colder than the space between stars, but that, too, is nature—and so are people.

The "beast" in "Storm Fear," suggesting the unfeeling and irresistible power of nature, has its counterpart in Stegner's fiction in many places, but perhaps most vividly in the animal imagery in his story "The View from the Balcony." In this story, a group of graduate students are having what was supposed to have been a celebratory party for Tommy Probst, a member of their group who was to have taken, and presumably passed, his doctoral exam earlier in the day. However, the party takes a grim direction, first, when they learn that Probst, filled with dread, walked out of the exam without taking it and, second, when one of the guests, a psychology professor, in the heat of the party's activity challenges and actually physically wrestles one of his advisees, Charley Graham, and at one point nearly throws him off the roof of the terrace on which the party is being held. The professor, Paul Latour, is described as having a "face . . . like the face of a predatory bird, beaked, grim lipped" (96), and the wrestling match takes on the air of some sort of animal ritual in which the older Latour is defending his leadership of the pack against a younger challenger. Latour tells Charley, "Given half a chance . . . you'd open your wolfish jaws and swallow me. You're like the cannibals who think it gives them virtue to eat their enemy's heart. You'd eat mine" (99). The contest, which begins as a sort of party game, gradually escalates to a real life-and-death struggle.

Later, sexuality, with animal-like overtones, comes to the fore when the wife of another professor is willingly carried off during the party by one of the students into the "jungle," the brush and trees surrounding the river below the terrace. These and other incidents emphasize the irrational, the animalistic, the primitive, which seems to really drive these people from what might normally be thought of as the intellectual and refined atmosphere of the graduate school. Indeed, a veneer of civilized normality stands in Frost-like ironic contrast to the episodes of the primitive in the story: the story takes place on the campus of a university in the bosom of American ordinariness, the Midwest—an odd place to find a "jungle" complete with animal sounds; and Charley Graham seems to be your typical all-American nice young man, but he reveals a determination, a "killer-instinct" that Tommy Probst lacks. Latour may not be so far off the mark in his assessment of Charley after all.[5]

Below the terrace on the other side of the river is the city zoo, and roars from the lions penetrate the darkness during the party, punctuating the ongoing displays of primitive human emotion. The roars are particularly chilling to Charley's British war-bride, Lucy, who during the course of the story becomes increasingly emotionally isolated from these ex-GIs, who are, with one exception, so smug in themselves and confident of the future. When the party breaks up, there is a search for the missing wife, and for an instant as Lucy looks out from the roof into the darkness below, she sees, in a flash of headlights from a car, a canoe on the river with a couple in it.

A moment later she finds it hard to believe that she saw what she saw. She even feels "a little knife-prick of terror that it could have been there—so silent, so secret, so swallowed in the black, as unseen and unfelt and unsuspected as a crocodile at a jungle ford" (104). Heat lightning flares, and she holds her breath waiting for the sound of thunder, but none comes. Instead, at that instant, the lion chooses to roar again. Her heart pounds as she thinks,

> What if he should be loose? . . .
> What if, in these Indiana woods by this quiet river where all of them lived and worked for a future full of casual expectation, far from the jungles and the velds where lions could be expected and where darkness was full of danger, what if here too fear prowled on quiet pads and made its snarling noise in the night? (104)

Her epiphany brings her to a realization that their sense of "normality," which has come out of their "fellowship of youth and study," and their common assumptions and hopes are "as friable as walls of cane" (105). Like the family in the Frost poem who find their sense of the ordinary diminishing in the darkness and mounting snow and become aware of the "beast," Lucy realizes that she and her friends, in their hearts, are actually "alone, terrified, and at bay, each with his ears attuned to some roar across the woods, some ripple of the water, some whisper of a footstep in the dark" (105).

Not all in these writers' works is ominous of course. As Stegner has said about Frost (and the same would seem to be true of the fiction writer as well):

> This is a poet who has always had a night and a day, a shadow and a sunshine, a spirit that can evolve out of bleakness and acceptance and a love of life, even the darkness in it. "Happiness Makes Up in Height for What It Lacks in Length," he says; in a stormy, stormy world he can get "the lasting sense of so much warmth and light" from "one day's perfect weather." ("Robert Frost" n. pag.)

Joy does come occasionally in human interaction with nature. There is the joy of work close to nature that we see in Frost's "Two Tramps in Mud Time," where the speaker is reluctant to give up his task of splitting wood to the two men who come looking for work. Or we see it in "Mowing" in the pleasure of doing a job right, of being engaged in the actuality of the work, so that the mower concludes:

> *Anything more than the truth would have seemed too weak*
> *To the earnest love that laid the swale in rows,* (25)

Similarly, the boy in Stegner's story "Saw Gang" finds satisfaction in performing his job well: "When Donald Swain breathed his lungs full of air, shifted his axe to the other shoulder, and said, 'Good workin' weather,' the boy looked at him and they grinned. It was what he had wanted to say himself" (70).

Often in Frost, moments of joy come when the speaker in the poem has a sudden apprehension of natural beauty, as in "Rose Pogonias," where the speaker and his companions discover "a thousand orchises" among the grass of a meadow. They "raised a simple prayer" that the mowers might spare this spot while the flowers still bloomed (19). In Stegner's "The Sweetness of Twisted Apples" joy comes to the wife when she discovers the deformed apples left hanging from the trees in an old orchard. She picks one, tries it, and exclaims with delight at her discovery—they are absolutely delicious. Her husband dismisses her enthusiasm and jokes about the Garden of Eden, but she decides to gather as many apples as she can to fill the whole back of their car and take them home for cider. The metaphor here, so similar to Frost's in "After Apple-Picking," of apples gathered as tokens of experience, suggests once again that the woman is open, able to get beyond surface appearances, and, unlike her husband, able to gather experience unto herself and savor it.

The women in Frost's poetry often have a similar propensity for sensitivity to their surroundings. There is the wonderful extended simile in "The Silken Tent," wherein a woman is compared to a silken tent that is

> *loosely bound*
> *By countless silken ties of love and thought*
> *To everything on earth the compass round,* (443)

As in the Stegner story above, there is in Frost also a sensitivity in the female that the male sometimes lacks. A familiar example can be found in "The Death of the Hired Man," where Mary works on her husband to get him to share her compassion for the hired man who has come to their farm to die, her feelings brought to the fore in this metaphor:

Part of a moon was falling down the west,
Dragging the whole sky with it to the hills.
Its light poured softly in her lap. She saw
And spread her apron to it. . . . (52)

Women had a special place in Stegner's life and work, beginning with his mother, Hilda, who protected him from a rough and abusive father, who encouraged him in his school work, and who was always there when the young Stegner needed love and support. Her life was difficult and unfulfilling. As a farmer's daughter of that time, all she wanted was to be able to settle down in a house of her own, to raise her two boys, and to be able to have friends. But her husband's frequent moves in his search for the "Big Rock Candy Mountain" (Stegner's metaphor for striking it rich) and his activities outside the law as a bootlegger made having friends and a settled life impossible. Nevertheless, she endured the loneliness and difficulties without complaint and worked selflessly for the comfort of the family and the success of her children. Wallace ended up thinking of her as a saint.

One of the most traumatic periods of his life came during his mother's illness and death from cancer. The illness struck when his father and mother were living in Los Angeles, and the father took the dying Hilda to their vacation cabin on Fish Lake in Utah, where Wallace joined them in order to help out. When the difficulty of caring for her and her pain became too much, they moved to an apartment in Salt Lake City. Then that big, tough man, who in Wallace's childhood had mocked him for being a weakling, took off, disappeared, presumably because he could not deal with his wife's condition any more, leaving Wallace to care for her until her death several months later. He never forgave his father. Many years after, in a tribute to his mother called "Letter, Much Too Late," he described those last moments:

Fifty-five years ago, sitting up with you after midnight while the nurse rested, I watched you take your last breath. A few minutes before you died you half raised your head and said, "Which . . . way?" I understood that: you were at a dark unmarked crossing. Then a minute later you said, "You're a good . . . boy . . . Wallace," and died.

"I knew," Stegner wrote, "how far from true your last words were" ("Letter" 23). Yet, he realized that no matter what he said to her now, he would never convince her that he was ever less than she thought him to be. She lives on, he declared, in his head: "Except when I fail to listen, you will speak through me when I face some crisis of feeling or sympathy or consideration for others. You are a curb on my natural impatience and competitiveness and arrogance. When I have been less than myself, you make me ashamed" ("Letter" 23–24). Just as Mary worked on Warren to bring out the best in him in "Death of a Hired Man," so too Hilda, with that special gift of sympathy often attributed to womankind, continued to work on her son's conscience.

In the 1960s, decades after his mother died, four women friends of whom Stegner was very fond also died of cancer, nearly at the same time. It was a terrible blow, a return of the cruelty of those months spent caring for the one whom he loved so much and who was in such awful pain. A poem by Robert Frost gave him comfort and some measure of strength in dealing with all these deaths, starting with his mother's. When she died, she had said, "Which . . . way?" In his poem "I Could Give All to Time," Frost in his last stanza answered that question for Stegner:

> I could give all to Time except—except
> What I myself have held. But why declare
> The things forbidden that while the Customs slept
> I have crossed to Safety with? For I am There,
> And what I would not part with I have kept. (447)

Stegner quotes this stanza in the prologue to his novel *Crossing to Safety,* and the central event of the novel is the death from cancer of Charity Lang, a character based on Peg Gray. Here in this final novel, Stegner's devotion to his mother, his friendship with the Grays, his attachment to Vermont, and his loving admiration for the best in Robert Frost all come together in a luminous whole.

··

CHAPTER NINE

"Eastering"
Wallace Stegner's Love Affair with Vermont
in Crossing to Safety

In February of the year that he died, 1993, Wallace Stegner celebrated his eighty-fourth birthday, after an incredibly productive career as a writer and teacher of writing and as one of our most honored authors. Although his fiction and nonfiction have dealt with many locations in the United States and around the world, he has become known as a writer concerned with western history, culture, and environmental health—indeed, reviewers have come to refer to him as the "dean of western writers." Born in Iowa and raised in western Canada and Salt Lake City, he lived his last forty years in the semirural foothills of the San Francisco Peninsula. Yet Vermont, where he and his wife had a summer home for several decades and which he described at length in his last novel, *Crossing to Safety,* was probably the location he loved the best.

One day before his death, while interviewing Stegner and his wife, I must admit I was a bit shocked to hear this writer, who had written with such affection about so many western locales, tell me that if he had to choose between his house in California and his place in Vermont, he would choose Vermont. His wife, Mary, added that when the time came, they would prefer to be buried in the town cemetery in Greensboro, Vermont.[1] In fact Stegner's ashes were spread among the ferns on the Vermont hillside where he and his wife had their summer home. For a writer who put such emphasis in his work on a "sense of place," such a preference says something to us about what the West became in his eyes—perhaps it is a declaration of defeat, a statement that the environmental battle is gradually being lost and that whatever we valued most in the West at one time is now irretrievably gone and can be recovered only in history and nostalgia.

That certainly seems to be the message of *American Places,* a collaboration with his son, Page, that came out in 1981. In talking about the West, but most particularly about crowded California, there is the sense that—to use Gertrude Stein's famous phrase about Oakland—there is no longer any "there" there: no connection with history, no sense of connection with one's neighbors or sense of community, no feeling of connection with the land or reverence for the natural. Living nine months a year on the edge of Silicon Valley, Stegner saw it all go, in a rising storm of population growth and greedy exploitation, year after year; and he made it clear, both in his essays and in such fiction as *All the Little Live Things,* that it was a painful experience.

Silicon Valley was once the Santa Clara Valley, a delightful region of orchards, as well as some vineyards, and truck farms. On a sunny day, one could see from high in the green foothills above where Stegner had built his home, over a valley filled with trees to the glittering waters of San Francisco Bay just beyond. Now the air is dense with smog, the roads are choked with traffic, and the farms are covered over by houses and industrial parks. Despite efforts to save it, the bay is badly polluted, a brown mess. When the Stegners first built their house, they could look out in the other direction, across the hills behind them, and not see a single light flickering in the darkness. In the years just before Stegner died, the area around his modest ranch-style house became dotted with obscene "castles." Suddenly, over just a few years, the Stegners found themselves surrounded by huge mansions on mini-ranch-size acreages, mansions usually inhabited by only two people or owned by absentee Asian entrepreneurs. That people would carve up his beloved foothills as an investment, not even bothering to live there, disturbed him immensely.

The contrast between his developing feelings about California and those about Vermont, a contrast that is touched on in several of his more recent writings and comes to a sort of climax in *Crossing to Safety,* would seem indicative of Stegner's values in general. In brief, Vermont "has watched humanity go by, and has recovered from the visit" (as he puts it in *American Places* [35]), whereas in California, development has run amok and all that is left are "remnants"—the wildlife is largely gone from the foothills, except for those animals, like the coyote, that can adapt to man and a loss of habitat. Throughout *American Places*, by the way, he admires most those habitats that have resisted human encroachments the most successfully: Vermont, where vegetation and animals have come back and where humans have won only a standoff with nature, and the Great Salt Lake, which has been so hostile to humans that it remains largely unchanged except by its own cycles of rising and falling.

If you come from the land of smog, gridlock, and the constant growl of bulldozers, as I do, one of the things you first sense about New England when driving through in recent years is how empty it is and how quiet it is. In a strange reversal of the western movement, it has become a place to go to find those things that the West was settled for, room to be yourself and grow. In that regard *Crossing to Safety* can be seen to trace this reversal, as the Morgans move from Berkeley, to Madison, to the promised land, the Garden of Eden, which is now on the East Coast in the renewed wilderness of Vermont (Stegner makes the connection explicit with a number of images taken from the biblical story). The novel is in this sense a story of "eastering," a reversal in which the West of myth and dream is now found where we might least expect it.

New England now has the wild forests and wildlife that the West is gradually losing, as well as the water most of the West has never had. In *American Places* Stegner comments that "All through our forty years' acquaintance with them and our many summers of living in one of them, we have watched the north woods working quietly and inexorably to reclaim themselves, or part of themselves" (38). The difference is that there are many places in the West where once the trees are clear-cut, they will probably never return. It is too dry and rocky, and once the meager soil is washed away, there is little chance for germination.

It was not just the landscape of Vermont that attracted Stegner but also the people, who are "neighborly, helpful, and quite astonishingly tolerant of difference and eccentricity. They judge a person primarily by how he or she works. All of them know who they are" (40). Knowing who one is, having a sense of the history of one's place, and knowing how one fits into the patterns of history, geography, and nature were always important to Stegner, as he testifies in such works as *Wolf Willow*. In *American Places* he tells about an old Vermont couple who live way out in the country. Their children have all moved away, and they are living a difficult life, alone. "But no one would have known from their talk that they found it hard to have no sons or daughters who wanted [the farm]. They accepted and endured as they had always done" (41). These are the virtues that Stegner always admired—neighborliness, helpfulness, tolerance, endurance, and above all, independence and hard work.

These are also the qualities we often associate with the western spirit, at least in the western myth of rugged individualism; but the quality that in Stegner's view has too often characterized the real West is the spirit of "get rich quick," an attitude that he mourned from *Big Rock Candy Mountain* onward and that later had its embodiment in Tom Weld, the developer in *All the Little Live Things*. But it was not just the Tom Welds of his native region that bothered him—it was a sense that the "dream . . . of easy gold at the hand of fey or elf," as Stegner's friend Robert Frost put it, had overtaken and become the dominant spirit of the West (Frost 25).

In *Crossing to Safety* the present action takes place at the Lang "camp," their summer home on Battell Pond, a fairly large lake in northeastern Vermont. The real-life counterpart of this lake is Caspian Lake, near which Stegner, his son, and many close friends, including the Grays (who are the models for the fictional Langs), have summerhouses and cabins. Over the hill from the Grays and the Stegners, a few miles away from Caspian Lake, is Long Pond, a lake that had no structures around it and where the two families would go to picnic. In *American Places* Stegner writes about Long Pond, comparing responses to the lake by Vermont and, hypothetically, by California—attitudes in each region that might lead to land stewardship or to exploitation:

> Up to now, it is the pond that has saved itself. But against speculators with money—Florida money, California money, Venezuelan money, Kuwaiti money, Mafia money, whatever kind of money—it is going to need some help. To a certain kind of eye, Long Pond's hushed remoteness might be transformed into a vision of a thousand shorefront summer cottages, each with dock and boathouse; and an inn with a bar, tennis courts, perhaps a nine-hole golf course where the Rutledge meadow used to slope down to the water's edge.

If Long Pond were in California, that vision would almost certainly come true. Since it is in Vermont, there is a chance that something better may happen. For there is something in Vermont—in its climate, people, history, laws—that wins people to it in love loyalty, and does not welcome speculation and the unearned increment and the treatment of land and water as commodities. Here, if anywhere in the United States, land is a heritage as well as a resource and ownership suggests stewardship, not exploitation. (48–49)

These comments seem to put the situation, as Stegner saw it, in a nutshell—"unearned increment" and "treatment of land and water as commodities" versus stewardship. What was important to him was not just friends (and *Crossing to Safety* is really a story of a friendship) or a local people whose habits of hard work he admired, but also their attitude toward the land as a heritage that should not be exploited. For it is not just the friendship that brings these two couples together in the novel, but also a place that has given meaning to their lives.

The title of the novel and the prologue quotation from the Frost poem from which the title is taken emphasize these values. The quotation is the last stanza from "I Could Give All to Time":

I could give all to Time except—except
What I myself have held. But why declare
The things forbidden that while the Customs slept
I have crossed to Safety with? For I am There,
And what I would not part with I have kept. (447)

These lines suggest a number of interpretations applicable to the novel. For one, they may refer to those things, nonmaterial, that in the long run matter most—family, friendship, generosity, love, responsiveness to beauty, having done one's best—that in a sense we can take with us into death. For another, they may refer to the novel's central character, Charity Lang, and her strong-willed insistence (even unto the irrational) on the worthwhile things in life as she would define them, her insistence, in dying, on doing it right, according to her own lights. She is someone who knows who she is but at the same time is always concerned about the welfare of others, always at pains to share. Perhaps the quotation refers to that which lasts, that which turns out in the long run to be worth holding on to. But most of all, the lines suggest to me a definition of life, that we must grab and hold on to it, and that we are truly alive only in the dynamic of bringing together independence and caring for others; and in this sense there is no one more alive in the novel than Charity.

Of course, Charity is not always right: her values are not always those that the narrator or reader would approve of. She is wrong in downgrading the importance of her husband's poetry writing in favor of his getting tenure as a professor. But as wrong as she is on occasion, Charity is usually a force for good, her generosity, love, and thoughtfulness overbalancing her occasional narrow-minded willfulness. The reader might see in her the mythic figure of the goddess with great potential for good or for ill, a potential powered by her nearly supernatural energy. (And Charity is almost larger than life in her dynamism.) What is most striking about her and her family is how closely tied they become to their environment (if she is a goddess, she is the goddess of Battell Pond) and how concerned they are about the preservation of the best values of their place—or to put it another way, how well they fit into their place as observers and participants in nature. There is a beautiful scene in the novel in which Charity and her husband are seen emerging, dripping wet, naked and unashamed, out of the water at dawn—an epiphany of beauty, love, and naturalness of man in nature:

> Then voices, male and female, just a word or two. I turn. The lake, obviously warmer than the air, steams. The island lies green in the lead-colored water. Out of its brush, splendidly naked, come Sidney and Charity Lang, picking berries into a metal saucepan.
>
> They are in sight only a moment, and they are intent upon what they are doing, and do not look my way. Standing in my startled goose-pimples, I watch them pick along the fringe of brush and out of sight again, glimpsed and gone, woods creatures. (159)

Charity and her family seek always to learn about, explore, and appreciate this country that, as the novel states it, is "romantically returning to wilderness" (149); and one of the points of the novel is how they bring their friends, Larry and Sally Morgan—the Westerners—into a similar relationship with these Vermont surroundings.

One might profitably compare the valuation of nature of the Langs and

Morgans with the attitude of Joe Allston in *All the Little Live Things.* Joe has retired from the East to what he calls an "authentic Eden," suburban California, to find that he cannot turn his "back for two days without having the place taken over by things that wither or curl or frazzle the leaf, things that feed on the hearts of roses, things like mildews and thrips and red spiders and white flies and mealy bugs and borers, the blights, the rusts and the smuts." He spends February through November employed "in a holy war against the thousand pests that infest Eden" (54–55).

By contrast, when Larry Morgan takes an early morning walk in Vermont, it is on "a road I have walked hundreds of times, a lovely lost tunnel through the trees busy this morning with birds and little shy rustling things, my favorite road anywhere. . . . I go alertly, feast my eyes, I see coon tracks, an adult and two young, in the mud, and maturing grasses bent like croquet wickets with wet" (5). He glories in the sight of "brown caves of shelter" for mice and hare, whereas Allston spends much of his time trapping, poisoning, and shooting moles, mice, and gophers. Morgan's garden is real Eden as defined by eyes of tolerance and love.

Like Allston, Charity in *Crossing to Safety* wants to bend nature to her own will and her own uses, a trait that the narrator calls the serpent in the garden of their experiences together. She is most right when she accedes, as in the birth of her child, to the natural rhythms of life, and most wrong when she tries, as at her death, to resist those rhythms. This resistance is most strikingly characterized by an episode in the novel when the Langs and Morgans go on a pack trip into the backcountry. Charity is bound and determined to follow a book on camping, literally, and a number of disasters follow, including a terrible few hours when the group, at Charity's insistence, follows a compass, rather than looking at the territory, and runs into an impossible timber fall. One might say that her greatest fault is that she often ignores her instincts and natural surroundings and attempts follow a compass through life, running into one barrier after another. That is, like the fortune hunters and exploiters that we find in Stegner's fiction, the bad side of Charity ignores the world around it to pursue its selfish aims. We are reminded through this, another duality like the Joe Allston–Marian Catlin duo in *All the Little Live Things,* that living rightly is often matter of seeing rightly. But the duality in *Crossing to Safety* is largely within Charity herself; she is one of those marvelous characters that Stegner was so good at depicting who force the reader into strongly ambivalent feelings about them. We love and admire Charity within nature, but we are irritated beyond measure with her when she tries to force nature—or the natures of her husband and friends—to conform to her own will. In her split, she is really the archetype of the good and the bad of humankind's potential in nature.

Crossing to Safety began, oddly enough, as a California novel. Stegner said that his original first chapter began in his house in Los Altos Hills, as he looked out the window at whatever wildlife was moving around (not much), in response to a phone call earlier that morning announcing the death of the model for Sid Lang, Charity's husband. Stegner had not gotten far with his first draft before he realized that "the people I was writing about were so New England, rather than Californian, that they wouldn't ever be anything but remembered exotics in this setting."[2] And yet, in another strange reversal of fact that contradicted Stegner's instinct, the real-life Langs *were* transplanted New Englanders who lived for many years in Southern California, but "in the story they couldn't be—they just felt out of place." They were out of place because, as Stegner frequently asserted, places do have a lot to do with the formation of character; and the kind of character and the values espoused—those demonstrably approved of in the novel—could not come out of a California lacking a sense of the past and with a future clouded by greed and separation from nature.

Crossing to Safety was published in 1987, six years before the author's death, and was his last novel. As such, and in that it combines his concern for the environment with his talent for creating rich, psychologically complex fiction, it might be taken as his last will and testament. The novel would seem to give testimony to those things that after a long life he came to consider most important: friendship, love, tolerance, and care for our natural surroundings. It is sad, however, in that it may also have been an announcement that he had given up on the West. The "easy dream" has won; and hard work, a firm sense of self and place, and a respect for nature would, in his mind, now belong to Vermont. That Eden is now in the East may be an irony that Westerners will find hard to bear.

CHAPTER TEN

An Introduction to Wallace Stegner's
Angle of Repose

Angle of Repose was Wallace Stegner's masterpiece, the crown jewel in a multifaceted writing career. From the time he received his doctorate in 1935 to his death in 1993, he published some fifty-eight short stories, a dozen novels, two histories, two biographies, a memoir-history, and five collections of essays. He was given numerous awards for his writings, including the Pulitzer Prize for *Angle of Repose,* the National Book Award for *The Spectator Bird,* and the Robert Kirsch Award for Lifetime Achievement from the *Los Angeles Times.*

Starting in the early 1950s, he became as well known for his environmental activities and writings as for his fiction. However, it was the writing of novels that was closest to his heart, and it was as a novelist that he wanted to be remembered. In a recent poll of readers of the *San Francisco Chronicle* regarding the best one hundred novels written about the West, *Angle of Repose* was listed number one. Often mentioned by critics as one of the most important American novels of the twentieth century, it alone should insure Stegner's reputation. (In a *Chronicle* poll of best nonfiction books, his John Wesley Powell biography, *Beyond the Hundredth Meridian,* was listed number two.)[1]

Wallace Stegner's life almost spanned the twentieth century, from the last homestead frontier in Saskatchewan to the information age in Silicon Valley, from horse and plow to mouse and computer. The major strands of his career, his love of the land, his concern for history, his advocacy of cooperation and antagonism toward rugged individualism, and his dedication to writing can be clearly seen as products of his parents' characters and of his early life. As we have seen, Wallace's recollections of growing up make it clear that a split developed early in his consciousness between the tough, intolerant rugged individualism represented by his father, the "boomer," and the tolerant, neighborly tendencies toward cooperation represented by his mother, the "nester." And as we see throughout his writing, Wallace's sympathies lay with his mother and the values she represented.[2]

Together his parents would seem to have been the archetypal western couple. In later years, as a writer, Wallace saw them as representing the exploiter on the one hand and the civilizer on the other. Although Oliver and Susan Ward are quite different in character and background, we can see them in their roles in *Angle of Repose* as dim reflections of Stegner's parents. (Certainly Wallace's deep love and respect for his mother contributed to his ability to create such complex and sympathetic women characters as Susan Burling Ward.) When asked by an interviewer if the life of Mary Hallock Foote, the model for the heroine of *Angle of Repose,* had reminded him of the life of Elsa Mason, the mother in the semi-autobiographical *The Big Rock Candy Mountain,* Stegner said,

> Not consciously. It never occurred to me that there was any relation between *Angle of Repose* and *Big Rock Candy Mountain* till after I had finished writing it. Then I saw that there were all kinds of connections. There was the wandering husband and the nesting woman, and the whole business reproduced in many ways in somewhat more cultivated terms and in different places what *The Big Rock Candy Mountain* was about. It's perfectly clear that if every writer is born to write one story, that's my story. (Stegner and Etulain 48)

Two periods in his growing up had a major influence on the formation of his outlook and interests. The first was his six years in childhood spent wintering in the village of Eastend and summering on the homestead farm in Saskatchewan near the Montana border. After the first year, his older brother Cecil had a summer job at the grocery store in town, and so Wallace was alone with his parents, out on the hot prairie, living in a tar paper shack. Yet, amazingly enough considering such a barren and hostile environment, he could still look back on a childhood not of suffering and boredom but of freedom and "a closeness to earth and weather" (*Wolf Willow* 29). His summers on the homestead and winters in the frontier village during his most impressionable years marked him, as he said, "a westerner for life." And these experiences would eventually produce a writer determined to represent the western experience as it really was and the relationship of western people to the land—as it was, is, and should be.

The crop on the homestead was wheat, and four years out of five the Stegners were dusted out. George, discouraged and angry at the elements, moved his family to Montana. This period in Eastend was the only time in Wallace's life that his family was together in their own home, and so having to leave Saskatchewan was for him a trauma he never forgot. Family, home, and community are valued throughout his work; and although Susan, in *Angle of Repose*, is on a much higher social level than Wallace's mother, Susan too is a nester who tries to create community wherever she must move in response to her husband's search for fortune in the West.

As we have seen, Wallace's sense of the importance of water in the West, which had been drilled into him so forcefully, led him eventually to write about John Wesley Powell—one of the few to understand the basic dryness of the West (contradicting the propaganda of the developers who promised a "new Eden"). And still later Stegner would use as the central episode in *Angle of Repose* Oliver Ward's attempt to transport water to the near desert of southern Idaho.

His experience in Saskatchewan also led him to a consuming interest in history. *Angle of Repose*, which is about the life and thoughts of a historian and the family history that he uncovers, would seem to have been written as much by a historian as by a novelist, and Wallace was both. As a child, so often alone, Wallace became an omnivorous reader, reading whatever came his way, even devouring the Eaton Catalog. But neither his education in Canada, which tried to make a European of him, nor his own reading in geography or history seemed to have any relevance to his own life or the place where he lived. The sense of his own lack of history grew in him as he matured, leading him to recognize the importance of knowing the history of one's own family and region. Later, in addition to writing histories and the memoir-history *Wolf Willow* that came out of an investigation of his own roots, he would do extensive historical research as a basis for several of his novels, including, of course, *Angle of Repose*.

The second important period in Wallace's early life would further support his passion for history and his interest in his roots. After leaving Saskatchewan, the family eventually ended up in Salt Lake City, where Wallace spent his teenage years. "The Mormons who built it and lived in it," he wrote, "had a strong sense of family and community, something the Stegners and the people they had lived among were notably short of." He was attracted not only by the Mormon emphasis on community and on cooperation but also by the Mormon devotion to the study of history and genealogy. In high school he made friends who brought him into the Mormon Church's activities—the dances, the basketball, and the Boy Scouts—and despite the dislocations caused by his father and a dysfunctional family, he came to believe that he could belong, that he was not an outsider. In later years he considered Salt Lake his hometown, and he chronicled his return home, rediscovering his youth, in the novel *Recapitulation.* So impressed was he by his experiences in Mormon culture that he wrote his two histories, *Mormon Country* and *The Gathering of Zion,* about the development of that culture.

A sense of community and a sense of family unity were not things, however, that he had in his own personal life during those years. His father, having given up wheat farming (with which he had planned to make a fortune because of the demand during World War I), turned to bootlegging and running a "blind pig," an illegal saloon in their home. The family moved some twenty times during Wallace's high school and college years in order to escape discovery by the police. This rootlessness, his mother's isolation, and the fact that he could not bring friends to his own home further reinforced his sense of the importance of family and community. Out of this background we can see reflected in *Angle of Repose* a concern for the effects of cultural transplantation, a concern for questions about what holds a family together and what drives it apart, and a concern for having roots, both in family and place, and knowing about them.

Wallace worked his way not only through college but through graduate school as well. He had a fellowship at Iowa that kept him in school after he had graduated from the University of Utah. After writing three short stories for his master's degree, his advisor, Norman Foerster, told him he should switch from creative writing and get his doctorate in an academic subject if he wanted to get a job teaching. Foerster further suggested that Stegner investigate the writings of the western naturalist-geologist Clarence Dutton, a figure out of the late nineteenth and early twentieth centuries, who had been largely overlooked.

By taking up this challenge, Stegner committed himself to what turned out to be a lifelong interest in nature writing. He would also develop a strong, continuing interest in that group of surveyors and geological explorers who after the Civil War mapped and described the West (including not only John Wesley Powell but also the real-life counterpart of Oliver Ward in *Angle of Repose*). And his dissertation topic led him to becoming an expert on the literature and history of the realistic-naturalistic period (from the Civil War to World War I)—the period that he concentrates on in the historical sections of *Angle of Repose*. He would go on to teach the literature of that period, the works of Twain, James, Garland, Wharton, Crane, and Dreiser.

He not only taught the standard fare but also spent much time in the library reading the magazines and journals of the period in order to get a better feeling for the times and to unearth new material for an anthology he was editing. While doing so, he discovered Mary Hallock Foote, the real-life counterpart of Susan Burling Ward in *Angle of Repose*. In the novel, Ward's true love is the most famous magazine editor of the period, Thomas Hudson, and as a result of his research, Stegner was quite familiar with the careers of nineteenth-century editors and with their magazines. Ward, like Foote, is seen in the novel as an illustrator and story writer, and her work, like that of her counterpart, is much in demand by the periodicals of her day.

Wallace had had no plans to become a professor; but it was the Depression, and there was hardly any place for him besides school. Nor had he had any notion of becoming a writer. After writing his dissertation about Dutton, getting his doctorate, and coming back to Utah to teach, he happened to see an advertisement for a Little, Brown novelette competition with a prize of $2,500. He was making only $1,800 a year as a professor and his wife, Mary, was pregnant. Almost with the desperation that leads us to bet on the lottery, he sat down and wrote a story he had heard from his wife about some of her distant relatives. The result was *Remembering Laughter*, which, much to the Stegners' surprise and delight, won the novelette prize. At that point, for the first time, he thought that writing as a career might be possible.

However, two undistinguished novels followed, and he was having more success with his short stories than his novels. It was not until he wrote the novel that told the story of his growing up, *The Big Rock Candy Mountain* (1943), that he had another success with the longer form. After having left Harvard, where he had been teaching writing as a Briggs-Copeland Fellow, he went to Stanford after World War II, where he began what became one of the most renowned creative writing programs in the country. He continued, however, to have more success with the short story (winning several O. Henry Awards) and with his nonfiction (including the Powell biography—a Pulitzer finalist) than with the novel. He was discouraged and thought that he might give up writing novels altogether.

A breakthrough did not come until late in his career, when he wrote *All the Little Live Things*. It was with this novel that he, at last, found his voice by inventing Joe Allston, the narrator who is witty, sometimes wise, and often cantankerous. Allston in *All the Little Live Things* would become the pattern for the narrators in Stegner's last novels and the forerunner in several ways of Lyman Ward in *Angle of Repose*. Allston was in part a product of Stegner's own reaction—now that he himself had grown older—to the late 1960s and its radicalism and to the blossoming of the "now" generation with its antihistoricism, intolerance, and hypocrisies. Sometimes this voice is light, even flippant in tone, entertaining, but always there is an undertow of skepticism.

With Allston, for the first time the novelist experimented with the first-person singular, which up to this point he had avoided. It seemed to him that "you couldn't deal with really strong emotions in the first person because it's simply an awkwardness for an individual to talk about his own emotions." But once he began to work with it, he found he could do things that he could hardly do by any other means: "First person narrative encourages you to syncopate time, to bridge from a past to a present. It also allows you to drop back and forth, almost at will, freely. When Joe Allston or Lyman Ward is working with the past, his head is working in the present" (Stegner and Etulain 76, 78). And time, this merging of the past with the present, is not only an essential aspect of structure in these late novels, it is in itself a central theme and of particular importance in *Angle of Repose*. During this period, with the onset of the Allston type of narrator, Stegner made a conscious effort to, in his words, "interpenetrate the past and present." In several essays he stated that his goal was to do for the West what Faulkner had done for Mississippi, that is, discover "a usable continuity between the past and present." And he added, "That's what western novels too frequently don't do" (Stegner and Etulain 78; "Born a Square" 179).

With Allston in *All the Little Live Things* and *The Spectator Bird*—and the narrators descended from him, Lyman Ward in *Angle of Repose* and Larry Morgan in *Crossing to Safety*—Stegner used a first-person narrator to achieve a voice close to his own, yet fictional. These narrators fit Stegner not only because he was getting older and matched them in age and perspective but also because these characters stood in strong opposition to the excesses of his times, to the nihilistic, self-indulgent, and self-centered attitudes we see expressed so often by the younger generation in *Angle of Repose.* Stegner said that one of the themes of *Angle of Repose* was this generation gap

> especially the antihistorical pose of the young, at least the young of the 1960s. They didn't give a damn what happened up to two minutes ago and would have been totally unable to understand a Victorian lady. I could conceive students of mine confronting Mary Hallock Foote and thinking, "My God, fantastic, inhuman," because they themselves were so imprisoned in the present that they had no notion of how various humanity and human customs can be. (Stegner and Etulain 88)

Early in the anti–Vietnam War movement, Stegner marched with the students, but later, when the demonstrations turned violent, he was revolted and could not understand how breaking all the windows on the Stanford campus could bring an end to the war. By nature Stegner was the antithesis of the in-your-face hatred and anarchy that surrounded him. He was a liberal politically but nevertheless a man of old-fashioned virtues—polite, courteous, kind—who applied a great deal of self-discipline to his life and who usually repressed the outspoken opinionatedness that his first-person narrators are likely to voice. Their opinions are likely to poke holes in any pretentiousness or self-righteousness they see around them (or to endorse any positive things that may be unpopular or out of fashion). They have an advantage in their search for and affirmation of the truth: their time is over and they have nothing to lose. To balance the penalties of aging, there can be a perverse pleasure in being candid.

I

Stegner first came across Mary Hallock Foote, the genteel nineteenth-century local-color writer and illustrator whose life became the basis for *Angle of Repose*, in 1946, just after he came to Stanford. He was doing research for a chapter to be included in the *Literary History of the United States* called "Western Record and Romance." He read several of her novels and story collections, as well as uncollected stories in their original magazine publication. He judged her "one of the best, actually; she was good and hadn't been noticed" (Stegner and Etulain 85). He took notes on her work and put one of her stories in his anthology *Selected American Prose: The Realistic Movement, 1841–1900* and included one of her short novels on his reading list for his American literature class. At the time he was probably the only professor in the country to be teaching Foote's work.

A GI student in that class, George McMurray, enthusiastically reported to Stegner that he had come across Mary Hallock Foote's illustrations and writings about New Almaden (in the Coast Range foothills near San Jose, California). He told Stegner that he had found out that Foote had a granddaughter living in Grass Valley, California (near the Empire Mine, where Foote's husband had been the superintendent). McMurray said that he was going to go up there and see whether he could get Foote's papers for the Stanford library, with the idea of possibly using them as the basis for a doctoral dissertation on her life and work.

The Foote family gave McMurray the papers on the understanding that he was going to publish from them and that he would supply typed transcriptions of the letters to the family. McMurray planned to do the dissertation under Stegner's direction, but a decade went by with no progress and McMurray finally gave up. During the mid-1960s, Stegner borrowed the transcriptions from the library and took them with him to his summer home in Vermont to read.

> Reading her quaintly 19th century letters, I thought her interesting but certainly not the subject of a novel. She lay around in my mind an unfertilized egg. . . . What hatched, after three years, was a novel about time, about cultural transplantation and change, about the relations of a man with his ancestors and descendents.[3]

He did not want to write a historical novel (as he commented on several occasions, western literature was too often "mired in the past") but a contemporary one, and as he thought about the story in the Foote letters, the thought occurred to him that perhaps he could link the two together in some way, so that the past was made part of the present. That, in turn, led him to look for the sort of narrator who had "tunnel vision," frequently thinking about the past and thinking about the present in terms of the past.

The perfect model for what became his narrator, Lyman Ward, presented itself to him in the person of Norman Foerster, Stegner's dissertation advisor at the University of Iowa, who had come to the Stanford campus to retire. Foerster, unfortunately, had been struck by a disease that had paralyzed his legs. With some sorrow about what had happened to his old friend, Stegner, nevertheless, put himself into Foerster's place—how would he, a largely immobile literary historian view the world? As the novelist has said, "We all have to have in some degree what Keats called negative capability, the capacity to make ourselves at home in other skins" ("The Law of Nature" 217). Here was the tunnel vision that Stegner was looking for.

Foerster did not provide a character—Stegner invented him, descended from Joe Allston—but a point of view, literally a position from which to view the world. In comparing Allston with Lyman Ward, Stegner noted that

> Allston and Ward are very different types. Allston is more emotional than Ward, less over-controlled. Lyman Ward is pretty uptight all the time. Joe Allston is likely to get drunk and disorderly and to wisecrack in the wrong places. He's another kind of character, but he has some of the same functions as a literary device. (Stegner and Etulain 76)

Observer and commentator, Lyman Ward, immobile, travels through time and space via his mind's eye, which of course is precisely what a novelist does. He is rendered immobile not just by his disease, which does allow him to move about in his wheelchair, but also by his attachment to place, his ancestral home, and by his obsession with his family's history. Both literally and figuratively, he lives in the past. While one cannot agree with Lyman's son, Rodman, that his father's investigation of the past is a waste of time, his devotion does seem extreme—except when one realizes that his devotion is not just to the past for its own sake; he is also looking for guidance in his present situation. The subject of *Angle of Repose* is the life of Susan Burling

Ward, but the essence of the novel is the evolving consciousness of Lyman Ward, her grandson.

The novel can be roughly divided into two parts. The first third of the novel deals largely with Lyman Ward and his experiences and thoughts about his life. Lyman's story and his character (a contemporary man who can understand and sympathize with a Victorian lady) frame the remaining two-thirds, which deal with his grandmother, whose state of mind is often conveyed to us by her letters to her eastern friend, Augusta. This Susan Burling Ward material, based on Mary Hallock Foote's papers, would bring accusations of plagiarism, charges of misuse of source materials, and even angry denunciation by feminists who claimed that a male writer had deliberately set out to destroy the reputation of an accomplished female artist. Some of the charges arose out of misunderstanding and miscommunication; some out of spite and, no doubt, jealousy.

Stegner had gotten to know Janet Micoleau, one of Mary Hallock Foote's three granddaughters, in Grass Valley through the husband of his secretary, Alf Heller. He visited the Micoleaus on several occasions while he was thinking about using the papers, and Janet encouraged him to do something with them, since her grandmother had been largely forgotten. She hoped that through Stegner's work, interest in her grandmother's life and work would be revived. When Stegner decided to go ahead with a novel based in part on the papers, Janet told him to use the papers in whatever way he wished. Stegner assumed that she, who had had custody of the papers, spoke for the family.

There probably would not have been any trouble if all the Foote family as a whole had been willing to become involved in dealing with the novelist and if Stegner and the Foote family had agreed on what they meant by "novel." What the Footes meant was explained by Janet's sister, Evelyn Foote Gardiner, when she stated in an interview: "I thought he would write something like Irving Stone's biographical novels. That he would invent conversations and all of that, but that he would pretty much stick to the facts of their lives."[4] Although he changed and added in order to create a plot which gave the novel its central drama and which would bring together the past with the present, he did stick pretty much to the broad outline of their lives. However, Mrs. Gardiner and those who have taken up her cause have complained that he used too much of Mary's life and too many of her letters, accusing him of "stealing" Mary's material in order to write a prize-winning book (Walsh).

The Foote family, in a reaction understandable perhaps but inaccurate, has expressed the view that Mary's letters composed a major portion of the novel. Stegner does quote (with some changes) from many of the letters (roughly thirty-five letters out of a total of five hundred). There are thirty-eight instances of letter quotation, of various lengths, for a total of approximately 61 pages in a book with 555 pages of text—that is, roughly 10 percent of the whole. As small as the percentage may be, however, there is no doubt that the letters are an invaluable part of the novel, borrowing the actual words of a real correspondence to give, as they do, a feeling of depth and authenticity to Susan Burling Ward's character. It was a brilliant tactic, but one that had ramifications that Stegner did not foresee.

When Janet asked him not to use real names, since he was writing a novel, Stegner used fictitious ones and went further in protecting the identity of his sources in his acknowledgments, "My thanks to J. M. and her sister for the loan of their ancestors." In addition, he included the disclaimer, "This is a novel which utilizes selected facts from their real lives. It is in no sense a family history" (*Angle* n. pag.). But Mrs. Gardiner has insisted that since he did not give specific credit to Mary Hallock Foote, as she felt he should have, his use of the material was an unethical act, close to plagiarism. Since he was following the family's instructions in keeping the source of his material secret, this is a very harsh and, it would seem, unfair judgment.

The situation became more complicated when Rodman Paul got in touch with Stegner, while he was working on the novel manuscript, to tell him that he, Paul, had obtained the backing of The Huntington Library to publish Mary Hallock Foote's reminiscences (Foote). Wallace agreed to read Paul's introduction and offered to show him the letters. But the whole idea of protecting the Foote name through anonymity was in trouble. He wrote to Janet, repeating the warnings that he had given before:

> As I warned you, the process of making a novel from real people has led me to bend them where I had to, and you may not recognize your ancestors when I get through with them.
>
> On the other hand, I have availed myself of your invitation to use the letters and reminiscences as I please, so there are passages from both in my novel. . . .

> You suggested that I not use real names in any of my book, since what I am writing is not history or biography but fiction. I agree with that. But if the reminiscences are now to be published, it won't take much literary detective work to discover what family I am basing this story on. . . . The question arises, must I now unravel all those little threads I have so painstakingly raveled together—the real with the fiction—and replace all truth with fiction? Or does it matter to you that an occasional reader or scholar can detect a Foote behind my fictions?[5]

He went on to offer to modify the language and change all the names; he asked her to let him know what to do about changes if she thought it necessary and, as he had before, offered to send the completed manuscript to her to read. Janet replied that she did not think changes necessary, nor did she feel it necessary for her to read the manuscript. Stegner asked if anyone else in the family would like to read the manuscript. The answer was no, the others were too busy with their own lives to take the time.

In his letters Stegner warned Janet several times that the book would not be true to all the details of the Footes' lives. "For reasons of drama, if nothing else," he wrote, "I'm having to foreshorten, and I'm having to throw in a domestic tragedy of an entirely fictional nature, but I think I am not too far from their real characters."[6] Despite his attempt to make sure that the Foote family had some idea of what a novel was and what he was writing, and despite his offer to make changes as dictated by Janet and his offer to let her or other members of the family read the manuscript, part of the Foote family took great offense at the book when it was published. They blamed Janet, who suffered deeply from their upset and anger, but most of all they blamed Stegner, who they believed, despite all the evidence to the contrary, had tricked them. The irony is that the novel with its Pulitzer and its controversy have brought more attention to Mary Hallock Foote than she would ever have received otherwise.

II

Using the Foote letters may have been a brilliant touch, but it not only caused him difficulties after the novel was published but also made its composition difficult:

> The novel got very complex on me before it was done. It gave me trouble: I had too many papers, recorded reality tied my hands. But a blessed thing happened. In the course of trying to make fiction of a historical personage I discovered, or half created, a living woman in Victorian dress. I forced her into situations untrue to her life history but not, I think, untrue to the human probabilities that do not depend on time or custom. In the end I had to elect to be true to the woman rather than to the historical personage.[7]

The novel is certainly a complex one, probably Stegner's most complex, yet at the same time it remains a book that is not only readable but a joy to read.

For one thing, it is a book of powerful, memorable characters. For another, it is a book with constantly building and engaging drama, dramatizing several important themes. It may seem odd on the surface that a novel with a central character bound to his wheelchair and to his home should have such drama. That drama is built through not just one but a series of connected conflicts within Lyman Ward. Although he is not a totally lovable character, he is a decent man who has had some bad breaks in life and whose thoughts engage us both by their wit and occasional profundity. Because of his disease and because his wife has abandoned him, he has reached a major crisis point in his life. "It would be easy," he thinks at one point in the novel, "to call it quits" (200). But he is a survivor, and as strange as it may seem, he is saved by his training as a research scholar, by his thirst for knowledge. His crisis leads him to the need to find a direction for his shattered life. That direction is provided by finding out about and trying to understand his grandparents, the events that shaped them, and the conflict between them; and his curiosity as it pushes ever forward becomes ours. It becomes the medium of suspense, holding us throughout. "What really interests me," Lyman tells us, "is how two such unlike particles clung together, and under what strains, rolling downhill into their future until they reach the angle of repose where I knew them. That is where the interest is. That's where the meaning will be if I find any" (211).

Another aspect of Lyman that leads us to empathize with him and holds us to his track of discovery is his vivid imagination. He is not only historian but also, in effect, novelist, bringing his characters and their interactions to life. Joseph Conrad was by Stegner's testimony a favorite author, one that he learned much from, and it was Conrad who said, "My task, which I am try-ing to achieve is by the power of the written word to make you hear, to make you feel—it is, before all, to make you *see*. That—and no more, and it is everything" (Preface 914). Through the talent of Wallace Stegner, Lyman Ward has the power to make us see. And if there is any one secret to the suc-cess of this novel, this is it.

A major pattern of conflict within Lyman and hence the novel can be cate-gorized under the past versus the present, more specifically at times, the old West versus the new. As Lyman thinks about his own situation, implicitly comparing it to that of his grandparents, we wonder how, facing so many obstacles to happiness, they are going to make it through life. As Stegner put it, "Since [Lyman's] own marriage has collapsed he's interested in this one that didn't, even though it had all the provocations that his had to fall apart" (Stegner and Etulain 94). But we also have a third pair, the contemporary marriage of the two flower children, Shelly and Larry Rasmussen. Altogether, three kinds of marriage: each in a different time frame, running from the past to the present. "'Progressive decline,' I would call it," the author stated (Stegner and Etulain 94).

Certainly, as Lyman tells us in the novel, this is a book about marriage, and just as certainly it reflects Stegner's own values in that regard. We might note that he remained happily married to the same woman for nearly sixty years. But we might just as well say that this is a book about forgiveness, also reflecting the author's values. While the marriage of Oliver and Susan remains intact, Oliver apparently never totally forgives his wife for her apparent infidelity and for possibly contributing to their daughter's death, doing so only insofar as he stays with her. Lyman wonders if he can even go that far in his own life and take back his wayward wife, Ellen.

One of the strengths of the novel is the complexity of its characters: their many-sidedness convinces us of their reality. These characterizations, along with the quoted letters and Stegner's vivid descriptions, provide a depth of realism seldom found in fiction. It is like turning from the flatness of regular TV to the multidimensional picture of HDTV. After reading and rereading this novel, it is hard not to lapse into the mistake of calling the central char-acter Mary—which may be a point in favor of the Foote family objections. Despite the negatives attached to the two major characters, we learn to care about them and follow their progress through the novel with concern. Like our feelings about Lyman, our connection to Susan grows despite a number of flaws—her snobbery, in particular, and her treatment of her husband. But our connection grows as we come to understand her, and it is Stegner's triumph that we do come to an understanding of this woman, this genteel, Victorian lady, so aloof, who would seem on first glance to be so foreign to contemporary taste.

But in so many ways she really is contemporary. Living in an age and stratum of society in which a woman could find the freedom to leave her family only by submitting to a husband and committing herself to his life, Susan remains her own person. Outwardly a captive, she is liberated from within and makes her way to success in the larger world. What she has in common with her grandson, Lyman, is courage and a strong sense of independence. After marrying Oliver, a civil engineer, she follows him west to one mining camp after another and makes the best of each situation, experiencing a way of life so different from the society she enjoyed in the East and regrets leaving. Lyman says of her,

> Susan Ward came West not to join a new society but to endure it, not to build anything but to enjoy a temporary experience and make it yield whatever instruction it contained. . . .
> . . . A modern woman in a mining camp, even if she is the wife of the Resident Engineer, lives in pants and a sweatshirt. Grandmother made not the slightest concession to the places where she lived. (81, 98)

Our connection to her is reinforced by Lyman's affection for her, although as the drama of her life unfolds before him, he often wishes he could take her aside and, knowing the future, warn her about apologizing for her husband and constantly comparing him unfavorably with more socially adept men.

Separated from the culture of the East, she keeps her connection by her correspondence with her friend Augusta, while at the same time exercising her talents for writing and drawing, becoming the best-known woman illustrator of her time. Not being able to enjoy the liberation provided by the feminist revolution, Susan Burling Ward goes beyond the modern woman by having liberated herself. There is connected to this, of course, the theme of the conflict between traditionally male and female roles and values, here exacerbated by the strains and extremes of western life. In the Wards we have to some extent the stereotypical nineteenth-century American man and woman—the man mostly silent and devoted to making his way in the world and the woman loquacious and socially conscious. Their complexity raises them above the stereotypes, but the basic conflict in roles and values remains.

Susan's husband, Oliver, is also a complex character, but since we see him only indirectly, he remains throughout a somewhat shadowy figure. We do know that he is quiet, competent, ambitious, and hard-working. After nearly five years of acquaintance, he proposes to Susan. He has been trying to make his way in the world to be worthy of her. He worships his wife in an old-fashioned way but is withal a man's man. Lyman calls him

> the silent character in this cast, he did not defend himself when he thought he was wronged, and left no novels, stories, drawings, or reminiscences to speak for him. I only assume what he felt, from knowing him as an old man. He never did less than the best he knew how. If that was not enough, if he felt criticism in the air, he put on his hat and walked out. (235)

His complexity comes only through Susan's reflections on him, which are decidedly mixed.

Before their marriage she is attracted to him because "he had an air of quiet such as she had known in men like her father, men who worked with animals" (38). But after their marriage she frequently compares him unfavorably with other men, particularly with Thomas Hudson, the man she would have liked to have married and who marries her best friend, Augusta. But even more overtly and painfully she compares him to her husband's assistant, Frank Sargent, with whom she falls in love. In reaction to all his failures, Oliver starts drinking, much to his wife's disgust:

> "Doesn't it humiliate you to think that you can't resist that temptation when someone like Frank, living out on the railroad with the roughest sort of men, never touches a drop? Why can't you be like Frank?" And that was the greatest mistake of all. "Because I'm not Frank," Oliver said, staring at her reflected face. "Maybe you wish I was" (435).

Lyman decides that Susan "must unconsciously have agreed with [her husband's] judgment that she was higher and finer that he. I wonder if there was some moment when she fully comprehended and appreciated him?"

(25). Oliver remains somewhat mysterious to us, almost mythic in stature. He suffers the slings and arrows of many misfortunes, both personal and professional, silently. One wound that has surely grown and festered over the years is his wife's disappointment in his inability to achieve the material success that would have raised them socially. But it is not that he cannot do his job well but that in his sense of duty he passes up opportunities in order to stay with his family and he is too honest to compete in the helter-skelter western world of get-rich-quick exploitation. At heart, Lyman tells us, he is a builder, not a raider.

Angle of Repose is a thoughtful book with a rich panoply of characters, both major and minor, and one that explores many themes, themes that bring the novel into the center of our culture. Like *The Great Gatsby* it helps us define who we, as a people in this new land, are. Oliver in his gallant romanticism is our Gatsby, and Susan in her own romantic snobbish world is our Daisy, and ne'er the twain shall meet until at the end they find their angle of repose. We have all, to use Fitzgerald's words, looked toward the "fresh, green breast of the New World," and we all believe, or would like to believe, in the American Dream, although we may each define that dream in our own way. We may, like Willie Loman, be defeated by the system or by our own self-delusions, but we can live and try go forward only if we believe. Our going forward, of course, often means going west, looking for the main chance, as Stegner's own father did, or as Bo Mason, the character modeled after George Stegner in *The Big Rock Candy Mountain* did, or as Oliver and Susan Ward did. East versus West, civilization versus opportunity, is a theme at the heart of the American experience. And as our boats beat ceaselessly into the past to find our future, we continue to ask, what have we inherited?

CHRONOLOGY

1909   Born February 18 at Lake Mills, Iowa. Lived in Grand Forks, North Dakota, and Redmond, Washington.

1914–1920   Lived in Eastend, Saskatchewan, in the winters, attending grammar school, and on a homestead near the Montana border in the summers.

1920–1921   Lived in Great Falls, Montana, and attended junior high school.

1921   Family moved to Salt Lake City, Utah, where they lived in twenty houses over the next ten years. Wallace attended East High School.

1927   Graduated from high school and entered the University of Utah at age sixteen. Played varsity tennis. Writing talent recognized by several professors, including novelist Vardis Fisher. Became editor of university literary magazine.

1930   Graduated from the University of Utah and took up a fellowship at the University of Iowa, where he became a teaching assistant and submitted three short stories for his master's thesis.

1932   Family moved to California, and Wallace enrolled in a doctoral program at Berkeley in order to be nearby his mother, who was ill with cancer.

1933   Left Berkeley when his mother's cancer worsened, and family moved to Salt Lake City, where his mother died.

1934   Continued studies toward Ph.D. in American literature at University of Iowa and took job teaching full-time at Augustana College in Rock Island, Illinois. Married fellow graduate student, Mary Stuart Page, in September. First professional publication of a short story, "Pete and Emil."

1935   Took a job as instructor at University of Utah and finished his dissertation on Clarence Earl Dutton, surveyor of the West and naturalist.

1937   Son Page born January 31. Gained first literary success with the publication of *Remembering Laughter,* which won the Little, Brown novelette prize of $2,500. Began teaching at the University of Wisconsin and started on *The Big Rock Candy Mountain.*

1938   Joined the staff at the Bread Loaf Writers' Conference, where he began friendships with Bernard DeVoto and Robert Frost.

1939   Wallace's father committed suicide in Salt Lake City. Appointed Briggs-Copeland Fellow at Harvard and began teaching in the writing program.

1940   *On a Darkling Plain,* first full-length novel.

1941   *Fire and Ice* (novel).

1942   *Mormon Country* (regional history and description). "Two Rivers" wins second prize in the O. Henry Memorial Short Story Award competition.

1943   *The Big Rock Candy Mountain* (novel).

1945   Took a leave from Harvard and went to work on *One Nation* for *Look* magazine. Shared Anisfield-Wolfe Award and received a Houghton Mifflin Life-In-America Award for *One Nation* (a series of essays on discrimination and prejudice in the United States). Appointed professor of English and director of the Creative Writing Program at Stanford University.

1949   Built home in Los Altos Hills, California.

1950   Won first prize in the O. Henry Memorial Short Story Award competition for "The Blue-Winged Teal." *The Preacher and the Slave* (novel) and *The Women on the Wall* (first story collection). Took around-the-world tour sponsored by Rockefeller Foundation.

1951   *The Writer in America* (essay).

1953   Took a trip to discover the history of his childhood region in Saskatchewan.

1954   *Beyond the Hundredth Meridian: John Wesley Powell and the Second Opening of the West* (biography-history). "The City of the Living" won O. Henry Award. Traveled to Denmark and Norway to discover family roots.

1955   *This Is Dinosaur* (edited collection of essays).

1956   *The City of the Living* (second collection of stories).

1960   Wrote "Wilderness Letter" (one of the most famous environmental declarations).

1961   Became assistant to Secretary of the Interior Stewart Udall. *A Shooting Star* (novel).

1962   *Wolf Willow* (history, memoir, and two short stories dealing with Saskatchewan). Began four years of service on the National Parks Advisory Board.

1963   Canadian Historical Association Certificate of Merit awarded to *Wolf Willow*.

1964   *The Gathering of Zion* (history), which won American Association for State and Local History Award of Merit. "Carrion Spring" won O. Henry Award.

1965   Elected fellow of the American Academy of Arts and Sciences. Rachael Stegner, granddaughter, born.

1967   *All the Little Live Things* (novel).

1969   *The Sound of Mountain Water* (first collection of essays). Elected member of the National Institute of Arts and Letters.

1971   Retired from Stanford as Jackson E. Reynolds Professor of Humanities and Director of the Creative Writing Program. *Angle of Repose* (novel).

1972   Pulitzer Prize for Fiction for *Angle of Repose*.

1974   *The Uneasy Chair: A Biography of Bernard DeVoto.*

1975   *The Letters of Bernard DeVoto.*

1976   *The Spectator Bird* (novel).

1977   Won National Book Award for Fiction for *The Spectator Bird*.

1979   *Recapitulation* (novel).

1980   Was first recipient of the Robert Kirsch Award for Lifetime Achievement from the *Los Angeles Times*.

1981   *American Places* (second collection of essays—with Page Stegner and photos by Eliot Porter).

1982   *One Way to Spell Man* (third collection of essays).

1987   *Crossing to Safety* (novel). *The American West as Living Space* (collection of lectures).

1988   *On the Teaching of Creative Writing* (collection of lectures).

1990   *Collected Stories of Wallace Stegner.*

1992 *Where the Bluebird Sings to the Lemonade Springs: Living and Writing in the West* (fourth collection of essays).

1993 Died, April 12, as a result of injuries sustained in an auto accident in Santa Fe, New Mexico, where he had gone to accept an award.

1998 *Marking the Sparrow's Fall: Wallace Stegner's American West,* edited by Page Stegner (fifth collection of essays).

NOTES

INTRODUCTION

1. James D. Houston, personal interview, Santa Cruz, California, January 10, 1990.

CHAPTER TWO

1. Thomas J. Lyon presents a different list of western realists, whom he calls "revisionists." He says,

> The first generation of "serious" or "literary" western poetry and fiction writers, beginning with Robinson Jeffers (b. 1887) and including Harvey Fergusson (1890–1971), Vardis Fisher (1895–1968), A. B. Guthrie, Jr. (1901–1990), and Frank Waters (1902–), were sharply aware of the received mythology of the West. Each strove for a realist's stance vis-à-vis his own personal history, and attempted to view larger historical matters with similar objectivity. . . . These writers did not view the West as an endless frontier; they did not make one-dimensional heroes of explorers, trappers, cowboys, gunfighters, and so forth; and they did not share the arrogance of Manifest Destiny. (144)

Vardis Fisher was one of Stegner's professors at the University of Utah, and A. B. Guthrie, who was a colleague for several years at the Bread Loaf Writers' Conference, became a good friend. When Stegner published *Wolf Willow* (1962) and sent a copy to Guthrie, Guthrie wrote to thank him and mentioned that he had been planning a similar book himself but that Stegner had beaten him to the punch.

2. The phrase "rugged individualism" seems to have been coined by Herbert

Hoover in *American Individualism* (1922) and entered the common vocabulary during the presidential election campaign of 1928. In a speech in New York City on October 22, 1928, he declared, "When the war [World War I] closed . . . we were challenged with a peacetime choice between the American system of rugged individualism and a European philosophy of diametrically opposed doctrines—doctrines of paternalism and state socialism" (*Oxford Dictionary* 105). Stegner uses the phrase in several ways, linking together the cowboy myth, the western attitude of independence and self-sufficiency (contradicting, in his view, the facts of western history), and the kind of ruthless and selfish entrepreneurialism that exploits both human and natural resources.

3. Of his older brother, Cecil, Stegner said, "He was always an athlete, he was always big and strong. He actually wound up not as tall as I am, but he was a kind of bull. . . . I was held to be smarter than he was, but I was such a runt he couldn't help being ashamed of me. Nevertheless we got on very well, and we were good friends." (Stegner and Etulain 11)

In 1930, when he was twenty-three, Cecil died suddenly of pneumonia. Wallace grew into a big, strong man and was something of an athlete in college, playing freshman basketball and for several years varsity tennis.

CHAPTER THREE

1. Stegner has written about this in many places, among them "Thoughts in a Dry Land" and "Living Dry," both collected in *Where the Bluebird Sings to the Lemonade Springs* (45–75).

2. See, for example, "The War between the Rough Riders and the Bird Watchers," "Variations on a Theme by Crèvecoeur" (on rugged individualism), and "If the Sagebrush Rebels Win, Everybody Loses."

3. Stegner moved to Salt Lake City when he was twelve (1921) and lived there until he graduated from the University of Utah in 1930.

4. Wallace Stegner, personal interview, Los Altos Hills, California, May 7, 1987.

5. "Wilderness Letter" has been reprinted many times, most recently in *Marking the Sparrow's Fall* (111–20).

6. Stewart Udall, personal interview, Phoenix, Arizona, May 22, 1989.

7. *The American West as Living Space* contained "Living Dry," "Striking the Rock," and "Variations on a Theme by Crèvecoeur," which were later also published in *Where the Bluebird Sings*.

8. A conversation between Wallace Stegner and Ansel Adams, videorecording, n.d., Stanford University Library Special Collections.

9. David Brower, personal interview, Berkeley, California, June 19, 1989.

CHAPTER SIX

1. "Bugle Song" was first published in the *Virginia Quarterly Review* 14 (July 1938): 407–15. It has been reprinted as "Buglesong" in *Collected Stories of Wallace Stegner*.

2. Mrs. R. E. Cameron, personal interview, Los Altos Hills, California, June 8, 1988.

3. "The Women on the Wall" was first published in *Harper's* 192 (April 1946): 366–76, and is reprinted in *Collected Stories of Wallace Stegner*.

4. The story first appeared in Stegner's *The City of the Living* and is reprinted in *Collected Stories of Wallace Stegner*.

CHAPTER SEVEN

1. Wallace Stegner, personal interview, Los Altos Hills, California, July 20, 1987.

2. Ibid.

3. For a discussion of several of the Bruce stories, see in this volume "The Battle against Rugged Individualism" and "Artist as Environmentalist."

CHAPTER EIGHT

1. Milton Cowan, personal interview, Ithaca, New York, August 4, 1986.

2. Theodore Morrison, personal interview, Amherst, Massachusetts, August 3, 1986.

3. Wallace Stegner, personal interview, Los Altos Hills, California, July 20, 1989.

4. Quotations from the poems of Robert Frost are documented by reference to page numbers from *Complete Poems*.

5. Stegner's Paul Latour was apparently modeled after the novelist Vardis Fisher (author of *Children of God*), who was Stegner's freshman composition teacher at the University of Utah. The occasion of the party is based on Fisher's short tenure at a summer session at the University of Iowa, where he lived in a fraternity house taken over for the summer by Stegner's graduate student friends (Flora 60–66).

CHAPTER NINE

1. Wallace Stegner, personal interview, Los Altos Hills, California, June 6, 1989.

2. Quotations here are from Wallace Stegner, letter to author, June 26, 1989.

CHAPTER TEN

1. For the fiction rankings, see "Acute 'Angle' Wins Reader Poll," *San Francisco*

Chronicle, November 11, 1999, n. pag.; and for the nonfiction rankings, see "West-Side Stories," *San Francisco Chronicle,* May 27, 1999, n. pag.

2. For Stegner's growing up, see "Finding the Place" and *Wolf Willow* (pt. 1).

3. Manuscript of an author's blurb for the *Literary Guild Magazine,* 1–2.

4. Evelyn Foote Gardiner, personal interview, Grass Valley, California, August 3, 1993.

5. Wallace Stegner, letter to Janet Micoleau, 1970.

6. Ibid.

7. Manuscript for author's blurb for *Literary Guild Magazine,* 2.

WORKS CITED

Abbey, Edward. *The Monkey Wrench Gang.* Philadelphia: Lippincott, 1975.

Bakhtin, Mikhail. *Problems of Dostoevsky's Poetics.* Trans. Caryl Emerson. Minneapolis: University of Minnesota Press, 1984.

Bonnetti, Kay. Interview of Wallace Stegner. Audio Prose Library. February 1987.

Cook-Lynn, Elizabeth. *Why I Can't Read Wallace Stegner and Other Essays: A Tribal Voice.* Madison: University of Wisconsin Press, 1996.

Davis, Lennard J. *Factual Fictions: The Origins of the English Novel.* New York: Columbia University Press, 1983.

DeVoto, Bernard. *The Letters of Bernard DeVoto.* Ed. Wallace Stegner. Garden City, N.Y.: Doubleday, 1975.

Dillon, David. "Time's Prisoners: An Interview with Wallace Stegner." *Critical Essays on Wallace Stegner.* Ed. Anthony Arthur. Boston: G. K. Hall, 1982. 47–59.

Fitzgerald, F. Scott. *The Great Gatsby.* New York: Charles Scribner's Sons, 1925.

Flora, Joseph M. "Vardis Fisher and Wallace Stegner: Teacher and Student." *Critical Essays on Wallace Stegner.* Ed. Anthony Arthur. Boston: G. K. Hall, 1982. 60–66.

Foote, Mary Hallock. *A Victorian Gentlewoman in the Far West.* Ed. Rodman W. Paul. San Marino, Calif.: The Huntington Library, 1972.

Forgacs, David. "Marxist Literary Theories." *Modern Literary Theory: A Comparative Introduction.* Ed. Ann Jefferson and David Robey. Totowa, N.J.: Barnes & Noble Books, 1984. 134–69.

Frost, Robert. *Complete Poems of Robert Frost.* New York: Henry Holt, 1959.

Guerard, Albert J. *The Triumph of the Novel: Dickens, Dostoevsky, Faulkner.* New York: Oxford University Press, 1976.

Hanscom, Leslie. "I Write the Kind of Novel I Can Write." [Interview with Wallace Stegner]. *Newsday,* March 11, 1979, *Ideas* section, 18.

Hepworth, James R. "The Art of Writing: An Interview with Wallace Stegner." *The Bloomsbury Review,* March/April 1990, 8–10.

James, Henry. *The Ambassadors.* Ed. S. P. Rosenbaum. New York: W. W. Norton, 1964.

———. *The Wings of the Dove.* New York: Dell Publishing, 1965.

Jefferson, Ann. "Structuralism and Post-Structuralism." *Modern Literary Theory: A Comparative Introduction.* Ed. Ann Jefferson and David Robey. Totowa, N.J.: Barnes & Noble Books, 1984. 84–112.

Kazak, Don. "What Wallace Writes." *Palo Alto Weekly,* May 2, 1990, 29–30.

Kirgo, Julie. "The Healing Country." *Vermont Magazine,* January/February 1993, 57–61.

Lodge, David. *After Bakhtin: Essays on Fiction and Criticism.* New York: Routledge, 1990.

Lyon, Thomas J. "Revisionist Western Classics." *Reading the West: New Essays on the Literature of the American West.* Ed. Michael Kowalewski. New York: Cambridge University Press, 1996. 144–56.

Mills, Kay. "A Look at the Real West." [Interview with Wallace Stegner]. *San Francisco Examiner,* August 20, 1977, n. pag.

Morrison, Theodore. *Bread Loaf Writers' Conference: The First Thirty Years, 1926–1955.* Burlington, Vt.: Middlebury College Press, 1976.

Olsen, Brett J. "Wallace Stegner and the Environmental Ethic: Environmentalism as a Rejection of Western Myth." *Western American Literature* 29 (1994): 123–42.

The Oxford Dictionary of Modern Quotations. Ed. Tony Augarde. New York: Oxford University Press, 1991.

Packer, Nancy. Untitled speech for Wallace Stegner's eightieth birthday celebration. Buck House, Stanford University, April 30, 1989.

Preface. "The Nigger of the Narcissus" in *The Great Critics: An Anthology of Literary Criticism.* Comp. and ed. James Harry Smith and Edd Winfield Parks. New York: W. W. Norton, 1951. 912–18.

Reynolds, Michael. *The Young Hemingway.* New York: Basil Blackwell, 1986.

Rideout, Walter, et al. Interview of Wallace Stegner. University of Wisconsin, May 1986.

Ronald, Ann. "Edward Abbey." *A Literary History of the American West.* Ed. J. Golden Taylor et al. Fort Worth: Texas Christian University Press, 1987. 604–11.

———. "Stegner and Stewardship." *Wallace Stegner: Man and Writer.* Ed. Charles E. Rankin. Albuquerque: University of New Mexico Press, 1996. 87–103.

Ross, Stephen M. *Fiction's Inexhaustible Voice: Speech and Writing in Faulkner.* Athens, Ga.: University of Georgia Press, 1989.

Schorer, Mark. "Technique as Discovery." *The Hudson Review* 1 (spring 1948). Reprinted [excerpt] in *Aspects of Fiction: A Handbook*. Ed. Howard E. Hugo. Boston: Little, Brown and Company, 1962. 168–170.

Shenker, Israel. "Whether the Short Story?" *New York Times,* November 20, 1970, n. pag.

Stegner, Page. "A Brief Reminiscence: Father, Teacher, Collaborator." *Wallace Stegner: Man and Writer*. Ed. Charles E. Rankin. Albuquerque: University of New Mexico Press, 1996. 27–33.

Stegner, Wallace. *All the Little Live Things*. New York: The Viking Press, 1967. Oxford, England: Basil Blackwell, 1986.

———. *The American West as Living Space*. Ann Arbor: University of Michigan Press, 1987.

———. *Angle of Repose*. Garden City, N.Y.: Doubleday, 1971.

———. "Battle for the Wilderness." *New Republic* 130 (February 15, 1954): 13–15.

———. "Beyond the Glass Mountain." Stegner, *Collected Stories* 21–31.

———. *Beyond the Hundredth Meridian: John Wesley Powell and the Second Opening of the West*. Boston: Houghton Mifflin, 1954.

———. *The Big Rock Candy Mountain*. New York: Duell, Sloan and Pearce, 1943. Lincoln: University of Nebraska Press, 1983.

———. "The Blue-Winged Teal." Stegner, *Collected Stories* 231–46.

———. "Born a Square." *The Sound of Mountain Water*. Garden City, N.Y.: Doubleday, 1969. 170–85.

———. "Buglesong." Stegner, *Collected Stories* 13–20.

———. "Butcher Bird." Stegner, *Collected Stories* 147–58.

———. "Child of the Far Frontier." Stegner, *Marking* 5–10.

———. *The City of the Living and Other Stories*. Boston: Houghton, Mifflin, 1956.

———. *Collected Stories of Wallace Stegner*. New York: Random House, 1990.

———. *Crossing to Safety*. New York: Random House, 1987.

———. *Discovery!: As Abridged for "ARAMCO World Magazine."* Beirut, Lebanon: An Export Book, 1971.

———. "A Field Guide to the Western Birds." Stegner, *Collected Stories* 311–59.

———. "Finding the Place: A Migrant Childhood." Stegner, *Where the Bluebird Sings* 3–21.

———. *Fire and Ice*. New York: Duell, Sloan and Pearce, 1941.

———. *The Gathering of Zion: The Story of the Mormon Trail*. 1964. Salt Lake City, Utah: Westwater Press, 1981.

———. "If the Sagebrush Rebels Win, Everybody Loses." *The Living Wilderness* (summer 1981): 30–35.

———. "In the Twilight." Stegner, *Collected Stories* 137–46.

———. "Lake Powell." *Holiday* 39 (May 1966): 64–68, 148–51.

———. "The Law of Nature and the Dream of Man: Ruminations on the Art of Fiction." Stegner, *Where the Bluebird Sings* 211–27.

———. "Letter, Much Too Late." Stegner, *Where the Bluebird Sings* 22–33.

———. "Literary by Accident." *Utah Libraries* 18 (fall 1975): 7–21.

———. "Living Dry." Stegner, *Where the Bluebird Sings* 57–75.

———. "Maiden in a Tower." Stegner, *Collected Stories* 267–78.

———. "The Making of Paths." Stegner, *Marking* 11–15.

———. *Marking the Sparrow's Fall: Wallace Stegner's American West.* Ed. Page Stegner. New York: Henry Holt, 1998.

———. *Mormon Country.* 1942. Lincoln: University of Nebraska Press, 1981.

———. "Oldest Americans." *One Nation.* Boston: Houghton Mifflin, 1945. 141–93.

———. *On a Darkling Plain.* New York: Harcourt, Brace, 1940.

———. "One-Fourth of a Nation: Public Lands and Itching Fingers." *Reporter* 8 (May 12, 1953): 25–29.

———. *One Way to Spell Man.* Garden City, N.Y.: Doubleday, 1982.

———. *On the Teaching of Creative Writing.* Ed. Connery Lathem. Hanover, N.H.: University Press of New England, 1988.

———. "The People against the American Continent." *Vermont History* 35 (1967): 177–85.

———. *The Preacher and the Slave.* Boston: Houghton Mifflin, 1950.

———. *Recapitulation.* Garden City, N.Y.: Doubleday, 1979.

———. *Remembering Laughter.* Boston: Little, Brown, 1937.

———. "Robert Frost: A Lover's Quarrel with the World." *Stanford Today* 133 (1961): n. pag.

———. *Robert Frost and Bernard DeVoto.* Stanford, Calif.: Stanford University Libraries, 1974.

———. "Saw Gang." Stegner, *Collected Stories* 69–74.

———. *Second Growth.* Boston: Houghton Mifflin, 1947.

———. "Sensibility and Intelligence." *Saturday Review* 13 (December 1958): 24.

———. *A Shooting Star.* New York: Viking Press, 1961.

———. *The Sound of Mountain Water.* 1969. Lincoln: University of Nebraska Press, 1985.

———. *The Spectator Bird.* Garden City, N.Y.: Doubleday, 1976.

———. "The Sweetness of the Twisted Apples." Stegner, *Collected Stories* 221–29.

———. "Thoughts in a Dry Land." Stegner, *Where the Bluebird Sings* 45–56.

———."The Twilight of Self-Reliance: Frontier Values and Contemporary America." *The Tanner Lectures on Human Values.* Ed. Sterling M. McMurrin. Salt Lake City: University of Utah Press, 1981. 193–222.

———. *The Uneasy Chair: A Biography of Bernard DeVoto.* Garden City, N.Y.: Doubleday, 1974.

———. "Variations on a Theme by Conrad." *The Yale Review* 39.3 (1950): 512–23.

———. "Variations on a Theme by Crèvecoeur." Stegner, *Where the Bluebird Sings* 99–116.

———. "The View from the Balcony." Stegner, *Collected Stories* 85–105.

———. "The Volunteer." Stegner, *Collected Stories* 293–309.

———. "The War between the Rough Riders and the Bird Watchers." *Sierra Club Bulletin* (May 1959): 4–11.

———. "We Are Destroying Our National Parks." *Sports Illustrated* 3 (June 13, 1955): 28–29, 44–46.

———. *Where the Bluebird Sings to the Lemonade Springs: Living and Writing in the West.* New York: Random House, 1992.

———. "Wilderness Letter." Stegner, *Marking* 111–20.

———. *Wolf Willow: A History, a Story, and a Memory of the Last Plains Frontier.* New York: Viking Press, 1962. Lincoln: University of Nebraska Press, 1980.

———. "The Women on the Wall." Stegner, *Collected Stories* 41–59.

———, ed. *Selected American Prose: The Realistic Movement, 1841–1900.* Toronto: Rinehart, 1958.

Stegner, Wallace, and the editors of *Look. One Nation.* Boston: Houghton Mifflin, 1945.

Stegner, Wallace, and Mary Stegner, eds. Introduction. *Great American Short Stories.* New York: Dell Publishing, 1957. 9–28.

Stegner, Wallace, and Page Stegner. *American Places.* New York: E. P. Dutton, 1981. Moscow, Idaho: University of Idaho Press, 1983.

Stegner, Wallace, and Richard W. Etulain. *Stegner: Conversations on History and Literature.* Reno: University of Nevada Press, 1996. Rpt. of *Conversations with Wallace Stegner on Western History and Literature.* Salt Lake City: University of Utah Press, 1983.

Walsh, Mary Ellen Williams, "*Angle of Repose,* and the Writings of Mary Hallock Foote: A Source Study." *Critical Essays on Wallace Stegner.* Ed. Anthony Arthur. Boston: G. K. Hall, 1982.

Watkins, T. H. "Typewritten on Both Sides: The Conservation Career of Wallace Stegner." *Audubon* (September 1987): 88–90.

Watt, Ian. *The Rise of the Novel.* Berkeley: University of California Press, 1962.

Wells, H. G. "He Is the Culmination of the Superficial Type." From "Of Art, of Literature, of Mr. Henry James." In *Boon,* London, 1915, 101–5. Reprinted in *The Idea of an American Novel.* Ed. Louis D. Rubin Jr. and John Rees Moore. New York: Thomas Y. Crowell, 1961. 248–50.